THE FIRST REALLY *NEW* PRACTICAL METHOD OF DOG TRAINING!

It is kind to your pet, quick, simple, easy and effective. The dog is not trained by force, but rather through his natural reflexes which are reinforced to encourage proper behavior.

With this system, you can teach your dog—in one gentle, easy, 15-minute session—more than you could pound into him in days of harsh training using the old, force methods.

The beagle which appears in the photographs inside this book was chosen at random. She was more than two years old, kennel bred, and had never been inside a house. Yet in a few short weeks she became a model house dog that not only behaved properly in every way but also could entertain when called upon and perform chores like bringing in the paper and carrying small parcels.

Of almost equal importance is the fact that this dog's trainer also had no previous experience. She is the author's secretary; with this book, she taught the dog everything from shaking hands to kneeling on command —all in simple 15-minute lessons.

Learn to better understand your dog—use your love for your pet to train him!

ANYONE CAN TEACH A DOG ANYTHING IF HE FOLLOWS THE ADVICE IN THIS BOOK . . .

Instill *positive* traits like—
- Becoming housebroken, easily and reliably
- Sitting when directed
- Standing or lying down
- Coming to you on command
- Carrying newspapers, magazines, slippers, etc.
- Avoiding certain household objects
- Shaking hands
- Becoming a watchdog
- Recognizing names of different objects

Eliminate *negative* traits like—
- Chasing cars
- Barking
- Shyness
- Animosity toward children, deliverymen, etc.
- Chewing objects
- Digging

And much, much more!

ABOUT THE AUTHOR

Dr. Leon F. Whitney is one of the best known members of his profession in the country. For a number of years he ran the largest veterinary clinic in the Northeast, now being run by his son. On the faculty of Yale University, he is also a consultant on animal feeding, and is active in research in animal medicine.

Dr. Whitney has written dozens of books on animal care and training, including "The Complete Book of Dog Care."

To
Friends of Animals, Inc.,
a humane, philanthropic organization;
and to the unselfish people who work
to achieve its purposes.

THE NATURAL METHOD OF DOG TRAINING

Leon F. Whitney, D.V.M.

AWARD BOOKS
NEW YORK

TANDEM BOOKS
LONDON

FIRST AWARD PRINTING 1969

AWARD BOOKS are published by
Universal Publishing and Distributing Corporation
235 East Forty-fifth Street, New York, N. Y. 10017

TANDEM BOOKS are published by
Universal-Tandem Publishing Company Limited
14 Gloucester Road, London SW7, England

Manufactured in the United States of America

Contents

Foreword

Deserve to be your dog's best friend

That was the eye-catching theme of Dog Week not long ago. It was backed up by practical, specific suggestions for dog-owners, and the most important of these, I think, was *train your dog*.

When I was in veterinary practice, I was amazed almost daily by the inexcusable misbehavior some of my clients tolerated in their pets. And when I talked to the owners about ways of training their dogs, I was often appalled by their lack of information—and even more, by the vast amount of misinformation many of them carried inside their heads.

True, there were those who had taken the trouble to get sound advice on training methods and had found time to apply it properly. Their dogs were well trained and well behaved. They were happy dogs. These people, I think, really *did* deserve to be their dog's best friend.

But those who hadn't the interest or knowledge or patience to train their pets—they were something else again. They were certainly not their dog's friend, nor did they deserve to be. In my opinion, they don't even *deserve* the dog.

"Why don't you train your dog?" I used to ask these people as they struggled with their spoiled and misbehaving pets. "It's easier than you think—much easier than what you are going through now."

7

The lazy ones, of course, found all sorts of excuses for *not* doing what they knew they should do. So I kept on patching up untrained dogs that had injured themselves needlessly. And I kept on listening as politely as I could to the owners' stories about how their dogs had chewed up the furniture, or had bitten the paper boy, or had become so demanding or so difficult to control that the owner couldn't even go away on a vacation.

As I look back now, I realize that I spent many hundreds of hours with clients explaining the simplest rudiments of dog training and suggesting ways that these fundamentals could easily be used to improve the behavior of their pets.

Remembering all this, I jumped at the chance when Mel Evans proposed that I do a book on training. We'd hunted coons together, and often, while the hounds were working the night woods around us, we talked about dogs and their abilities and how they could be trained. "Write a book that any dog-owner can understand and use," he said. "Not a technical book, but one that actually shows how anyone can apply the method you use. A book with plenty of specific examples and lots of pictures."

That's what I have tried to do here, and I think this is the kind of book he wanted. I know that it will do more for the reader than my talks did for my clients—for like all vets, I was always pressed for time. I'm afraid, too, that the people I talked to often forgot much of what I tried to explain to them even before they got their pets home.

Many people have helped with this book. Margaret Berna offered many valuable suggestions as she typed the manuscript. As the model teacher she showed admirable patience and understanding.

Stephen Hodio, who took the pictures, tackled a difficult assignment with enthusiasm. He adjusted his schedule to fit the training routine and was the soul of amiability—even when everything went wrong.

My wife has endured this book patiently as she has others in the past. She read and heard and criticized the various sections as they were written. And she even permitted her living room to be used as a classroom and studio. She has all my gratitude.

And Phoebe, too. She tried hard, worked happily, learned to face the flash bulbs stoically. At this writing she is expecting a family. May all her pups be as bright and cooperative as she.

L.F.W.

Orange, Conn.

The session is only ten minutes old, but the student seems to have mastered the assignment of the day.

The *Natural* Method of Dog Training

CHAPTER ONE

Be My Pupil

People have been keeping dogs and breeding dogs and training dogs for thousands of years. And, particularly within the last fifty years or so, they have learned a great deal about them. They have learned how to breed them selectively, how to feed them properly, how to prevent disease, and how to cure it. Dog-owners have found dozens of ways to use modern scientific knowledge and methods in the care of animals.

But, strangely, they don't seem to have learned very much about how to improve the old ways of training their dogs. Most of them are still using the same methods that their great-great-grandfathers used centuries ago. They still think that the best way—or the only way—to train a dog is to *force* him to do what they want him to do.

Today we know—or should know—that the *force method* is not the only way to train a dog. And certainly it is not the best way.

Force *will* work. It has been working for centuries. But it is slow, difficult, and often unnecessarily harsh.

There is an easier, quicker, better way to train dogs.

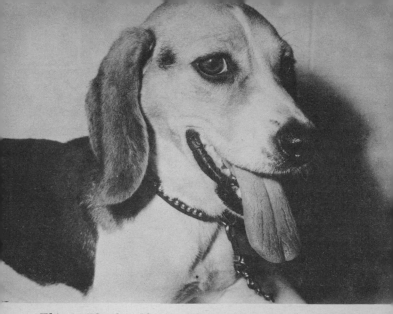

This is Phoebe. She is a pretty little Beagle, the willing scholar who posed patiently for the illustrations.

I call it the *natural training method*. Natural, because it puts to use in the most direct way the dog's native instincts. Working with the same reflexes by which he would be guided in a wilderness, this natural way of training conditions your dog to you, his master and friend, and to good behavior in our man-run civilization. It works well and easily because the trigger that sets off the reflex is the incentive to fill a need, not threat or punishment.

Instincts, conditioning, incentives—does this sound like the beginning of a book on animal psychology?

It shouldn't, because that isn't what the book is about. It's simply and solely a book about what I have found to be a new and better and easier way to train your dog.

It *is* true that the method is based on the fundamentals of animal psychology. As a veterinarian, I've had to study dogs, to learn not only about their physical nature, but also how they react and respond in various situations.

There is nothing special about Phoebe. Any one of these or a hundred other kennel mates might have done as well.

I've written many articles and even a few books about dog psychology.

You could, if you wanted to, also make a study of dog psychology. It is no more difficult than any other study, and—to my way of thinking—a good deal more interesting than most.

But I assume that you are not especially interested in that particular field of knowledge. You simply want to be able to train your pup to behave decently and be a good family companion. You can't spend day after day, month after month, at the job, but neither can you have an unruly nuisance about the house. You don't want to be rough or cruel with the pup, but you also realize that just letting him go his own way is going to end up in a long battle with more smacks and shouts than you like to think about.

I was a practical dog-trainer long before I was a veterinarian. I've trained hundreds of animals—from coon

13

hounds to Bloodhounds. With most of those dogs, I am now sorry to say, I used the old *force* method. I can promise you this: the *natural* method is not nearly as hard as the old method. It is easier, quicker, kinder—fun for both you and your dog.

You *will* need to understand a few of the principles on which the method is based. But only a few. In less than half an hour you can get through these few pages of general background information. After that, you'll be ready to start to work intelligently with your pup.

It occurred to me not long ago that training a dog is a good deal like learning to drive a car. If you had the time and interest, you could find out everything that goes on under the hood. But you don't. You merely push a few buttons and levers and pedals and the car responds. Mechanics and engineers know what happens with the machinery, but you don't know, and don't need to know in order to drive.

Learning isn't all classroom work. A good relationship between the teacher and the pupil is equally important.

Training a dog is much the same thing. You don't work levers on the animal, but you can learn an effective, simple method to produce the kind of behavior you want from him. With time and effort and strength, you can *force* a dog to do what you want him to do. If you were well-muscled enough, you could also push your car up a hill so that it would roll down the other side.

But why? Why do it the hard way when you can use the built-in responses of the dog to train him by the *natural method*? It's as simple as that.

So be my pupil. Learn to train your pup the *natural* way.

This book concerns two dogs in particular—*your* dog and Phoebe.

Pictures of Phoebe enhance nearly every page of the book. They are the real record of the actual beginning of her education.

Our student just happened to be Phoebe. Any other dog would have done as well, and some might have been better.

Phoebe is a pretty little Beagle. But she is nothing special. She is just one of scores of dogs that I keep in connection with a research on feeding. She is like all of the others—no brighter or slower of wit than any other pup I might have picked. She is, I would think, quite typical of the smallish house dog kept as a pet in hundreds of thousands of American homes.

The only thing different about Phoebe is that she knows a few things that most dogs her size and age don't know. She has learned to behave properly, to obey quickly and happily, and to do a dozen or so little tricks. How they were taught to her, how quickly and easily she learned them, you will see as you follow her through the book.

There is one other difference about Phoebe. She learned her lessons despite the photographer peeking around her teacher's shoulder and flashing his disconcerting lights at her at unpredictable moments.

Her teacher is Margaret Berna. Mrs. Berna is not a professional dog-trainer. Indeed, this is the first animal she has ever trained. But she did begin with one advantage. She is my secretary. She had not only read this book; she had also typed every word of it. She knew the principles on which this training method is based, and she learned how to apply them as she went along.

If training Phoebe looks pleasant and quick and easy as it is recorded here, it is only because it *was* pleasant and quick and easy.

You can prove it.

You can do the same thing with your dog.

CHAPTER TWO

Learning to Work
with Your Dog

We can assume that you and your dog are on good
friendly terms. You may have raised him yourself, or, if
not, you've had him long enough to get well-acquainted
with him and he with you. You will need to develop this
basic relationship before you start your training routine.

People often think that the way to begin is to establish
a "friendship" with their pup. To an extent that is true.
But there is an implication of equality in the word that I
don't like. Dogs are not human beings. If you begin by
thinking of your dog as a person, you are off on the
wrong foot.

To me a better term for the relationship you should establish is *rapport*—a *harmonious* or *sympathetic* relationship. It is a better word because it is more realistic and
more precise. It means simply that you and your dog get
along well and properly, that both of you understand and
appreciate your rightful positions.

How do you establish this necessary rapport?

You may enjoy petting your dog, but he would rather have you help him dig out the mole he has just found.

First of all, you must realize that every dog possesses traits that make him a natural member of the wolf pack from which he is descended. He is basically a cooperative creature, but in your household he has no group of dogs to associate with. He would like the companionship of other canines, but he is willing to adopt you as a more or less satisfactory substitute. But remember, *he wants to do things with you.* This is the crux of your whole relationship.

Those who idealize dogs will often tell you that because of his nature your dog loves to please you. That's a doubtful statement any way you interpret it, and only partially true at best. When he seems to be trying to please you, your dog is actually trying to fill a natural need of his own—the need for companionship. That he pleases you is only incidental. It is his own needs and pleasures that cause him to behave the way he does.

Doing something with a dog is the only real way to develop a sound rapport with him. It is true that by sitting in the living room with a pet dog, by feeding him, and combing him and brushing him, you can elicit some friendly feelings. But this kind of passive relation is not nearly as effective as a more active one. Even taking a walk with your dog is a whole lot better than sitting at home and petting him—aside from the fact that both of you probably need the exercise. If he sniffs out a mole in the park or chases a squirrel up a tree, you have your chance to build a sound relationship. You can work with him to dig out the mole. Or you can pretend to help him catch the squirrel by throwing a bit of a stick up into the branches of the tree. The thing is that you have *done* something with him. He'll respond. He's anxious to have you as a member of his pack.

There's another thing to consider. Every dog pack and every wolf pack has a leader. All the members respect his leadership. There are only two in your pack. Your dog wants and needs a leader, and you had better live up to his expectations. You get to be a leader not by petting and stroking and coaxing. You become a leader by *doing*.

This is all very elementary to people who regularly work with dogs. They know how important this rapport is —and how easily it can be established. To create this kind of understanding, you don't have to *live* with your dog. Professional dog-trainers often work with a dozen dogs day after day. I've known bird-dog kennels to have as many as fifty dogs in training at the same time.

Ask any hunter. I've owned hunting dogs of various kinds for most of my life. (Too many, sometimes.) A few years ago when I had incautiously gone off somewhere to lecture about some aspect of dog care or feeding or training, my wife went out to take a look at my Redbone and Beagle hounds in the kennels. Kate counts well—faster and better than I do. When she got up to a hundred, not counting the pups and about-to-be pups, she went back to the house to compose *her* lecture to me. I had a reasonable defense, of course—that research job on dog food —but we subsequently decided that the job could be done with fewer dogs and smaller ones. That's why Phoebe is the star of this book.

This is a long digression for a short book, but it *does* have a point. My assistant regularly fed the dogs and took care of them. I hunted with them. Now, where I live you can't go tramping over the hills with twenty or thirty dogs. I had to select only three or four. When I came out

Even a little indoor game is better than a sedate daily stroll—or a long, sleepy evening of television.

You don't have to keep romping with your dog. He will be just as happy to relax with you sometimes.

to pick the dogs that were to go on the hunt with me, the kennels invariably boiled with jealousy, with dogs barking and climbing all over each other to attract my attention. Those left behind were often frantically eager to follow. One regularly climbed out of a small six-foot-high wire enclosure. Another gnawed his way through tough boards. Several dug their way through rock-packed earth to escape.

Why? Not because they were lonesome. Not because I fed them or petted them or even spent much time with them. They fought to go hunting with me because they remembered previous hunts—because they wanted to be members of the pack.

I could give you dozens of examples to prove the point. Suppose a hunting dog is shipped to a new owner hundreds of miles from his old home. The new owner can spend hours and days petting him and feeding him and

21

making friends with him. But if he lets him out, there's a better than even chance the dog will leave and be lost.

But if the new owner takes him hunting—only once, perhaps—the dog will very rarely stray. He has joined a new pack.

You are probably not a hunter. But the moral still applies. *Work* with your dog. *Do* things with him. *Teach* him.

You will find that with every outing and with every lesson you will have a better and more responsive dog. Give him the chance to be part of your pack. That's the way to establish rapport.

If you want an alert, responsive, and happy dog, you will work with him—do things with him, teach him.

CHAPTER THREE

About Needs and Reflexes

We're going to have to talk a little about the theories underlying the natural method of training, and the time to do that is right here at the beginning.

If I push a dog's rear-end down and tell him soundly, "Sit!" and keep on repeating the performance, he will eventually learn to sit at my command. Haven't I trained him? I have. But have I trained him in the best way? Was it the easiest way for the dog and for me? No, I don't think it was.

I think the *natural method* is better. As a matter of fact, I think I can show you how to do the same thing in much less than half the time—while you sit in your chair and never say a word to your dog. We'll come to that a little later.

The first fact to remember is that *your dog's behavior is never uncaused*. He doesn't blink his eyes, turn his head, bay on a fox track, shake hands, roll over, get up and stretch, eat, bark, or do anything unless there is cause for it. With him, it is all cause and effect.

There are countless reasons why your dog acts the way he does. He *smells* an odor and reacts to it. He *tastes* bitter food and spits it out. These are instinctive reactions. He *hears* a noise and responds by barking. He *feels* excessive heat and draws away from it. He feels the pressure of a man's hand on his hips and sits. These are responses to what we might call mechanical stimulation. The thing to keep in mind is that your dog never does anything without a cause.

A harder thing for many dog-lovers to remember is that a dog does not and cannot think as human beings do. I know that many fine people think otherwise. But they are wrong. If they can demonstrate that any dog really *thinks,* all psychologists will have to make an abrupt revision of their concepts.

Every dog starts life with a great many native, inherited reflexes that have nothing whatever to do with his training. As he grows up, new patterns appear. But always he behaves in ways he doesn't choose and can't help. At first his reflexes are few and simple. At birth he is blind and deaf, but when his nose gets the odor of his mother's teats, he nuzzles one and opens his mouth. And when his tongue wraps around the teat, he sucks. When milk runs into the back of his mouth, he swallows. When his stomach feels full, he stops feeding. That's not much, but it is crucial.

When he is cold, he cries; when hurt, he screams. When he smells certain odors or has food in his mouth, the saliva flows. These reactions are native, completely independent of training. If he is a hound dog, and happens to smell an animal's trail, when he's a little older, he will run along it and bark or bay. If he is one of a so-called *mute* trailing breed, he will follow the trail silently. Training has nothing to do with this behavior—not at first, certainly. It is a natural response to external facts— as natural as a baby's crying when a diaper pin pricks him.

A reflex is defined as an *involuntary, invariable, adaptive response to a stimulus*. And if you have never thought much about reflexes before, this definition takes some explaining.

Of course you've seen your foot jump forward when the doctor tapped your knee while you were sitting with your legs crossed. The action was *involuntary*. In other words, you didn't will it, and you couldn't have prevented it if you had wanted to.

And every time you are struck on that particular spot, your foot jumps forward. The action is *invariable*.

The *stimulus* is the doctor's rubber hammer.

The *response* was your reaction to the blow.

Adaptive. Well, that simply means most of the reflexes we are born with or that develop as we grow older are there to help us survive and reproduce. If we couldn't adapt, we would perish as a species.

The same applies to dogs.

I have already mentioned several kinds of reflexes. Here is an illustration of another that can easily be demonstrated in human beings. Suppose you and I sit on opposite sides of a table. Between us is an electric light. We darken the room. What happens to our eyes? The pupils become enlarged—they dilate—a simple reflex over which we have no control at all.

If I press a button and light the bulb, then what happens? Our pupils contract. Another reflex—invariable, uncontrollable.

The light is the stimulus.

But suppose that as I press the button and light the bulb, I also say "contract." You hear the word. This accompanies the stimulus. We go through the exercise of switching the light on and off in the room thirty or forty times and every time the bulb lights, you hear the word "contract." What will have happened to you? You will have, to some degree, been *conditioned*. I can meet you two weeks later on a dark day when your pupils are fairly widely dilated and if I say *contract,* your pupils will do just that.

Dog-training is as simple as that. A *conditioned reflex* differs from a natural reflex in that it is acquired by repeated association or training. All training is the conditioning of reflexes.

This is important, for it explains the essential difference between the old system of dog-training and the natural system that I am advocating here. The old method depends on force or some modification of it; you force a dog to do what *you* want. The new system uses the *dog's* wants which you condition to your needs.

It is obvious, then, that if you are to be successful in training your dog by the natural method, the first thing you must do is to get him in a condition where he needs something. What are some of his needs? The need to escape, the need for companionship, the need for sex fulfillment, the need for sleep, the need to satisfy thirst, the need to satisfy hunger. These are among his simplest needs. Of all of them the most useful to the trainer is the dog's need to satisfy his hunger. And that is the one we shall use to train Phoebe.

CHAPTER FOUR

Using Incentives

You already understand that the secret of training your pup quickly and easily is simply to use his needs for your purposes. What you will have to do is to couple one of those needs (as an incentive) with an effective method of conditioning his reflexes. When you have done that, you are ready to start educating him.

Your dog has many needs that can be used as incentives. Food makes your dog happy. He's delighted to be scratched. He's grateful for a bowl of water on a warm day. And he is reassured, at least, by the friendly tone of voice that means he's on the right side of you.

These things he "understands." He reacts to them as incentives. Though there are many incentives, only a few are of any practical use for training purposes, and these often are misunderstood. It's worth taking a closer look at a few of them.

Incentive: Love to Please

A dog, as we have already said, does not love to please you. He cooperates with you to please himself. He *does*

Your dog has many needs, many incentives. By using them wisely, you can train him easily, quickly, permanently.

love to have you become what we have called a member of his pack. He cooperates with you that way, finds real pleasure in it, and so fulfills one of his needs. But that isn't as selfless as it looks. He adores company. Once he and his owner have taken to each other, he dislikes being left out.

This *love-to-please* response was the kinder side of the force method of training. "Good dog" and a friendly pat were thought to be rewards enough for obedience. They worked, but they worked slowly and inefficiently. You will find, as I have, that more tangible incentives produce quicker results. Of course, you should add to them a show of pleasure when your dog performs well. That's a part of his conditioning, too. Look out, though, that you don't confuse him with too many words. He responds to the tone of your voice, not only to the words themselves.

Incentive: An Itch to be Scratched

How do you make friends with a strange dog? People who don't know much about dogs almost invariably pat and stroke them. People who really understand them take hold of the base of the dog's ear and massage or scratch the skin. The dog that is merely petted probably will stand there. Stroking certainly doesn't hurt, the tone of your voice is encouraging, and there's always a chance that a satisfying scratch will develop out of all that smoothing. But a good vigorous scratching will get a much better reaction, often a comfortable grunt of appreciation.

Remember the last time the barber gave your scalp a good massaging? Your dog enjoys that feeling, too. Scratching your dog's head and ears certainly won't keep your fingernails clean, since you'll collect a bit of the wax that he secretes to keep his coat healthy. But he won't notice, and the wax washes right off.

Incentive: Hunger

There's no question about the incentive of hunger. Finding his food and consuming it was, of course, almost the first thing your puppy could do. And his interest in food has only grown livelier since then.

Hunger is the best incentive for our training method. It is easily produced, and just as easy to satisfy. Thousands of studies have proved it. Your dog will prove it again.

About the only basic question I have ever had from people who want to use the natural training method is that they are kind-hearted and they object to "starving" a pup. Let's clear that up right here. You are *not* going to "starve" your pup. The simple fact is that being hungry is not painful to him. It is hardly even unpleasant. He is not a human being and his food needs are not at all the same as yours. The thing you must remember is that he does not have the same kind of feelings that you have.

29

Look at it this way: The dog is a direct descendant of the wolf—an animal that lived then, as it does now, a feast or famine existence. These wonderful wild dogs often live for a week or more with no food at all. And so far as I know, nobody has ever suggested that these prolonged fasts in any way undermine the health of a wolf. Their bodies are adapted to that kind of irregularity.

In the same way a dog can easily live on nothing but water for a week—and in these days of overfeeding, many of them, in my opinion, would be the better for it. There are records of dogs that have lived more than a hundred days on nothing but water.

So let me repeat, you are *not* starving your dog. Normally, I suppose, you feed him once a day. If you postpone his regular feeding for another 12 hours, he will be 36-hours-hungry instead of 24-hours-hungry. That's not

Two minutes before the end of the training session Phoebe is still interested, still ready to continue.

starvation. For him that is nothing more than what I call *comfortable* hunger. He doesn't feel it any more than you do when dinner is an hour later than usual—if he feels it that much. Surely he doesn't experience anything comparable to the hunger pangs you have known at the beginning of a reducing diet. And even they are not nearly as severe as they are sometimes thought to be.

These are the facts, and you must accept them as such. I know something about the subject because I have worked on the problems of dog nutrition for many years.

It is a curious fact that animals of all sorts train most easily when they are 36-hours-hungry—more easily than if they have been fasted for 24 hours or 48 hours. I don't know why. But I do know that I have always found that a 36-hour fast is ideal with dogs.

So with Phoebe we have used the 36-hour schedule. You should do the same with your pup. The way it works out means that you can have an effective training session every other day. If you feed your dog Monday morning, he'll be ready for a lesson Tuesday evening. During the session he will have had a goodly number of tidbits and at the end of it will get the balance of his meal. Wednesday morning he gets his usual ration, and by Thursday evening he is ready for his classroom work again.

This is a practical, workable schedule. It is easy for the pup and should be reasonably convenient for you. He will enjoy it and so will you—and you can keep it up until one or both of you run out of time or ideas.

CHAPTER FIVE

Using Signals

When you train your dog—that is, when you condition his reflexes—you are going to have to teach him to recognize certain signals. Now, almost anything will serve this purpose. The signal may be a word, a toot on a whistle, a snap of a cricket (one of those five-and-dime clickers), the sound of a food pan being set on the floor, a key being inserted in a latch, a salty taste in food, the spoor of a fox—any sound or odor or taste, or other influence which gets through to one of the senses.

A little girl who lives in a house on a busy thoroughfare near me often sings out, "Daddy's coming!" when daddy's car is still nowhere in sight. How does she know? Because the family dog pricks up his ears and runs to the front window. We say that he recognizes the sound of the family car. It would probably be more accurate to say that he recognizes some special quirk in that motor, some special squeak so high in the sound scale that it is inaudible to human beings That tiny squeak is a signal to him.

*This is the beginning of a training session. Phoebe is
ready, waiting for the signal from Maggie.*

I know of another dog that pays no heed to the footsteps of the man who regularly delivers milk to the house.
But when the milkman goes on vacation, the dog sets up
a furious barking every time the substitute comes up the
walk to set the same bottles on the same steps outside.
Why? Different footsteps are different signals.

Sight signals are just as effective. Our little house dog
races to the front door as soon as he sees his mistress
begin to change her clothes. He's learned that when she
gets dressed up, the chances are good that he will go for a
ride in the car—which he loves.

Anything will work as a signal, but it is usually easiest
for you to use words. Your dog can develop a sizable recognition vocabulary. Tests have shown that he can learn
up to at least four hundred words, and unless you plan to
make a genius of him, that should be ample.

33

We are a little way along in the lesson now, and Phoebe is beginning to understand what the teacher expects of her.

What you are doing is using a recognizable sound to trigger an appropriate action by your dog. Make it simple. Keep it quiet. I want to caution you especially that you need not use a loud sound as your signal. If you begin yelling your word signal, you will have to continue to shout in order to produce the action you want. If you whisper the signals, they will be just as effective. But then you will have to continue whispering, and that is not always convenient. It is generally best to use a normal speaking tone.

Establishing this comfortable volume is for your convenience, not the dog's, though yelling, of course, would make you both uneasy. The ability of a well-trained dog to pick up and follow a signal that is all but imperceptible to us is amazing. Such a dog once thoroughly baffled me and a group of animal psychologists at Yale. His trainer told us he could count—and he did. We offered him several problems. He answered them, barking out the solutions. Apparently he was able to add, subtract, multiply, and divide.

None of us could detect any signal from the trainer. But just to make sure, we had him stand on one side of a screen while the dog, still "counting," was on the other. Finally the trainer explained his secret. A key word was the signal which started the dog barking. A very faint clicking sound which the trainer made with his tongue against his cheek was the signal to continue. When the clicks stopped, so did the barks. We had stood within three feet of the trainer and never heard the clicks. But the dog heard them.

This brings me—in an oblique sort of way—to something that has annoyed me for years. When I was a practicing veterinarian, I was amazed that the vast majority of people, when they approached a barking dog, for some reasons used the same identical phrase. "What's the matter?" they said. Nothing was the matter, of course. But I suppose that if they really could have comprehended, thousands of dogs would have been convinced that "Whatsthematter" was their name.

What's the matter? is meaningless to dogs—as, indeed, it is to the people who use it. As a signal for some action it is too protracted, not sharp enough or terse enough. There is too much conversation, even in such a short question. If the dog were taught to react to the signal "mat," which he easily could be, then the phrase "what's the *mat*ter?" would make sense to him. Once he learns to react to any signal, if it is a word, that word can be mixed in a rambling sentence and the dog will still react to it. Suppose he knows what "fetch" means. You can say "fetch," or you can say, "Listen here old boy, I want you to run over by the fence and fetch the ball." You let him

35

go and he fetches it. But do understand that all the verbiage except the word "fetch" was meaningless to him.

Please try to use only short words or signals with your dog. And when you greet a strange one, ask the owner the dog's name and greet the dog with that.

Years ago I had to make many calls on farmers, most of whom kept cattle dogs and watchdogs roaming around their places. What do you suppose would have happened when I got out of my car and a suspicious, unfriendly dog approached, if I had asked "What's the matter?" Nothing good. I used to sit on the car's running board (yes, it *was* some time ago) and command in a stern voice, "Come here!" This always had the desired effect. Only his owner had called him that way in the past. The words were enough to flip the switch. The dog then treated me as one of the family.

Signals are no problem. Pick ones that are brief, easy, distinct. Then just stick with them until they flip the switch.

CHAPTER SIX

Using Reinforcements

Some pages back I said that you could teach your dog to sit—without saying a word to him and without moving out of your chair. This seems to be the time to show you how to do that. I think that if I were you, I would be eager to be *doing* something with my dog by this time. You should feel the same way, and I hope that you do. This is also a good time for this first little lesson because it is a brief, neat illustration of the ways you can use your dog's needs—coupled with adequate reinforcements—to train him. This is a kind of extra used here merely as an illustration to help explain the principle of natural training. Later on you will learn an even quicker method.

This simple example includes all of the factors we have been talking about, all of the elements you will be using in the training of your dog. The natural method of training is no more than the intelligent use of reflexes, needs, incentives, signals, and reinforcements.

If you are going to teach your dog to sit on command, here is one way of doing it.

Until you are certain that the habit pattern has been permanently established, reinforce every correct response.

First of all you will need a place that is relatively quiet —as far removed as possible from sights and sounds that will distract your pup. I assume that he will have been fasted for 36 hours and that he will therefore be comfortably hungry. He then has a need—hunger—and he has reflexes. It is your job to use incentives and a signal in a way that he can understand. When you do, he will respond—probably a good deal more promptly than you expect.

Hunger, of course, is the incentive, and food the reinforcement. (We'll talk about the kind of food you are going to use in a minute or two.) You sit in your chair with your pup's feeding dish on the floor beside you. And since I promised that you wouldn't have to say a word, this time we will use one of those dime-store clickers (a cricket) as a signal. The sound serves as the equivalent of a word.

Without speaking to the dog or touching him, while he is looking at you, snap the cricket and drop some food in the dish. He will see it drop, come to the dish, and eat it. Then he will back away and look at you. Snap the cricket and drop another bit of food. Repeat this several times to give him an opportunity to associate the clicking sound with the food.

Now—wait until he has turned away and snap the cricket again. If he turns instantly and goes to the dish, he is ready for the "sit" training. If he doesn't, repeat what you've already done. But the cricket-food association will probably be accomplished in short order. I have used this method scores of times, and it has rarely taken more than three or four minutes to establish the connection between the sound and the dropping of the food.

You have partially conditioned your pup—and that *is* just what you've done when the sound of the cricket means food to him. Wait, then, until he sits. When he does—and *as* he does—snap the cricket and hand him a bite of food. Wait until he sits again, and then snap the cricket and give him another bite. Do this every time he sits. He will soon learn that the click, which means food and satisfies his need, happens only when he sits. Then, of course, he'll sit when he hears the cricket, for the cricket has become his signal. The food you give him is the "reinforcement." In one surprisingly short and easy session you will have taught your pup to sit without having said a word to him.

Now, what are these tidbits, these *reinforcements,* that you will be using? Many people think of them as *rewards,* and, indeed, for many years I considered them rewards myself. But actually they are *not* rewards. They are much more accurately described as reinforcements—and there *is* a real difference.

Let's make a simple analogy. On a fairly calm day a sailboat with an experienced skipper can cover a very considerable distance. The boat is propelled only by little, almost inconsequential gusts of wind. But each gust moves the boat forward a little bit, and each one adds something to the work that the preceding one has done. In an hour or so the boat will have crossed the lake or the bay simply because it has been able to use the reinforcement of every little puff of wind.

The tidbits that you give your pup work in precisely the same way. Each one adds something to what has already been accomplished. Each brings you a little closer to your objective.

Naturally, the food reinforcements that you use will be only a tiny, partial satisfaction of the need that your pup feels. Your job is to teach the dog to associate the satisfying of his need (hunger) with certain signals which you give him. The signal must be paired with the action. And if you satisfy his needs too quickly and too completely, he is going to lose interest in your program for the day, and you are going to have an unproductive session with him.

Another thing that needs to be stressed is the importance of *proper timing* during training. Take as an example this method of training your dog to sit. You have the tidbits, the dish in which to drop them and the cricket. You *must* drop the tidbits and snap the cricket simultaneously—and at first while the dog is looking at the food. (He probably smells it, too—and that's a help.) If you drop the food into the dish and wait half a minute before you snap the cricket, your pup almost certainly won't pair the sound with the reinforcement. If he doesn't, your lesson will have been a failure.

The timing of signal, reaction, and reinforcement must be very close. If more than five seconds elapse between them, your efforts will usually produce meager and disappointing results. Repetition is equally important. The successful conditioning of your dog depends on your willingness to repeat the signal-reaction-reinforcement routine at least thirty or forty times. With the old force-training

40

Once your dog has been properly conditioned, a pat and a friendly word is all the approbation he needs.

method, dog-owners often found it difficult to go through the disciplinary steps over and over again. And when they didn't repeat them, their training sessions amounted to little more than an inconclusive battle between man and beast.

The natural method is far more pleasant and much less arduous. But still the proper responses must be repeated again and again until the patterns become habitual. Your dog will learn quickly, and the temptation is always to stop the lesson too soon. Remember that you can't do any harm by repeating the lesson a few times more. But you can lose everything by stopping before the job has really been done.

While we are discussing this subject, we might take another practical example. Suppose that you want to teach your dog to retrieve a ball when you throw it. I hope you will, because it has a most practical purpose. Walking your dog around the block gives *you* a little exercise. But for your dog the exercise is hardly measurable. He could run miles while you are sauntering around the neighborhood. In most urban districts you can't let him run free. Nor are you likely to come home from the office and take him for a three- or four-mile run on a leash. But in many areas you *can* find a place where you can let your dog off his leash and let him race back and forth retrieving the ball you throw for him. Fifteen minutes of that will do him (and you) more good than all the hours of sedate pacing you could possibly spare. In my opinion, teaching your dog to "fetch" is almost the most creative thing you can do with him.

Most dogs can be taught this retrieving trick, but it will be a lot easier if you have one of the breeds that are natural retrievers—a Springer Spaniel, for example. The object is simple and clear. You want to throw a ball as far as you can, and you want your dog to find it, bring it back, and drop it at your feet. This is the way you do it.

You toss the ball a few yards away. He's after it, picks it up, and runs around with it. That's not really the idea. What you need now is a signal and a method to teach him to return to you with the ball when he hears that signal. For our signal, this time, we'll use a special whistle. It is called a Galton whistle, and it is calibrated so that it can be set to various pitches. We'll set it high. The dog can hear it, but it won't disturb humans. For reinforcement, have a handful of those tidbits we still haven't talked about. With whistle and tidbits—signal and reinforcement—you are ready to train your pup to fetch.

The dog still has the ball in his mouth, and he still isn't sure what to do with it. When his running brings him toward you, toot the whistle and drop some food at your feet. When he sees the food, he will come for it. In order to eat the food he will, of course, have to drop the ball.

That's what you wanted. If you do this three, four, or five times, you will have educated him to a small degree. But two days later he won't remember a single thing about your game. But if you do it thirty or forty times, he will have learned his lesson permanently and well.

All through this book, I'm afraid, I will be stressing the importance of repetition—repeating myself in order to force the habit of repetition on you. The point is crucial, and I don't apologize for it. When your dog responds quickly—as he often will—you will be inclined to skip those last ten or twelve repetitions. It seems obvious that he doesn't need them. But let me urge you: He *does* need them. If you neglect them, you will not establish the pattern firmly enough. And if you don't, you'll have to put him through his paces all over again. So—carry the session a little beyond what seems to you sufficient. You can't do too much. It is easy to fail to do enough.

We've talked about two sample lessons here. I hope you will try them with your pup. They have worked beautifully for me and for hundreds of other people.

But they don't *always* work that easily with *all* dogs. I'll give you an embarrassing example: Later on you will see pictures of Phoebe retrieving. Maggie tried to teach her to retrieve tennis balls, sticks, a rubber ball with a bell inside, a turkey wing. It didn't work. Phoebe, for some reason, didn't like tennis balls, sticks, or any other object we tried.

So, at the next session, I tried the old professor approach plus a little inventing. Now she will retrieve whatever we throw and tell her to *fetch*. Sticks, boards, knots of rope, newspaper folded up, a shoe. But Phoebe at first absolutely refused to be interested in tennis balls, baseballs, softballs, croquet balls, or any other kind of balls that we could think of. You will see her retrieving a stick. Until she learned the word fetch and its meaning, she would have nothing to do with balls.

You ask me why? The answer is simple. I don't know. All I can say is that not all dogs can be easily trained to do all things. Any dog can be trained to do many things. No dog, I believe, can be trained to do everything that another dog does. It is almost impossible to train a Pointer to put his nose ·to the ground and follow scents as a hound dog does. The moral is that you should make the most of your pup's natural aptitudes, and unless he is the right kind of dog for it—a Poodle or American Fox Terrier, for example—forget about the circus tricks.

By now, I hope you will have at least three or four questions in mind. Let's take them in their probable order.

First, you want to know about what kind of *reinforcements* to use. Food, of course. But what kind of food?

Well, it depends on you and your dog.

There was a time in my life when I was passionately interested in Bloodhounds. I trained dogs that are still being used by the police departments of some of the New England states. I shipped Bloodhounds abroad—to Israel, England and to other countries. Some of them have made famous news stories. To tell the truth, I wrote a book called *Bloodhounds and How to Train Them*.

For years I went along with the usual methods. In training my dogs I used half-inch sections of frankfurters which the dogs nibbled from my fingers. In those days I thought of these tidbits as *rewards*. As I have said, I think of them now as *reinforcements*. The point is that I deliberately fed the dogs a drab, daily wholesome diet— and for training I used the franks as tasty morsels that would encourage and buttress the kind of activity that I was trying to develop.

Today I'm not so sure that my old methods were sound.

There has been a lot of research in the field of animal psychology since I worked with Bloodhounds, and much of it indicates that the best reinforcement you can use is

You can train your dog when he is a pup. You can also ignore the cliché and teach an old dog brand-new tricks.

the food your dog likes and customarily gets. Some experts think that dabs of his regular food work better with a dog than special tasty bits. Since tidbits are especially palatable, the everyday meal will be pretty humdrum in comparison, and when it is offered to the dog at the end of the training session, he may well refuse to eat it.

There are many excellent complete dry foods which dogs relish, and on which they thrive. No food supplements of any kind need to be added to them, for they are really complete rations. All you need to add is water. Some are meal, and others are kibbled foods. Several companies manufacture kibbled foods and biscuits that are made of the same ingredients, and I have found that food which comes in these two forms is ideal for training purposes. The kibbled food serves as the regular diet. Biscuits, broken in half, make excellent reinforcements.

If you use canned food for your dog's regular diet, I hope that the one you are using is nutritionally complete. But that is beside the point here. Canned food is usually pretty sticky, and it is an unhandy kind of stuff to carry in your pocket. If your dog has been fed on canned dog food, I suggest that you boil some slices of beef liver, cut

45

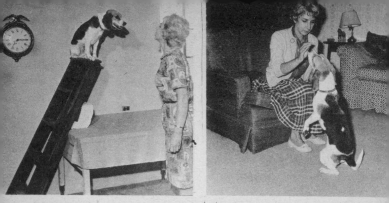

Phoebe looks youthful. But all of her training, as you see it here, was done after she might have been a grandmother.

them into ½- or ¾-inch cubes, and use these for reinforcements. You can put the liver in one of those handy plastic bags, put the bag in your pocket, and your training sessions will all be very neat and antiseptic.

One question that nearly ever new dog-owner asks is at what age he can or should train his dog. That is one that can't be answered by a simple figure.

To take the easier part—when can you train your dog? If you have in mind the chestnut about the impossibility of teaching old dogs new tricks, my advice is to forget it. I can assure you that your dog would have to be really senile if he failed to respond to the natural training methods suggested in this book. I think that you will agree that Phoebe looks and acts quite girlish. But she was three years old when these pictures were taken—and she turned out to be an excellent and cooperative pupil.

But you are more likely to want to know how *soon* you can begin the training program. For your own convenience you will at least want to have your pup housebroken as early as possible, and in the last chapter of this book you will find specific advice on that problem. You *can* teach a six-week-old pup to respond to signals. And there are advantages to starting that early.

46

Phoebe learned slowly but very well. Here she is delivering the newspaper—the proudest little news girl on our block.

Very early impressions are important to all puppies. For example, a puppy taken from its mother at the age of three weeks and handled a great deal will usually prove a better pet than an unhandled one taken at ten weeks. Early training is possible and sometimes desirable.

However, there are several factors to consider. It makes a difference whether you are training your dog in the rudiments of good household behavior, or whether you are teaching him things which depend largely on his innate, inherited behavior patterns as a basis for your training. A little earlier I indicated that it is easier to train a natural retriever such as a Spaniel, a Poodle, or a Labrador to retrieve than a dog of a breed never developed for retrieving. I also mentioned the difficulty of training a Pointer to follow scents with his nose.

Suppose you plan to teach a hunting dog to work the job for which his breed was developed—to train your Beagle, let's say, to run rabbits. What you should do is to learn when these aptitudes begin to appear naturally, and start your training then. Beagles, for example, start trailing rabbits when they are about four months of age. Tree hounds show their natural propensity of barking up trees at game quite a little later—at about eight months.

The real question here is perhaps not so much when you *should* begin to train your dog as when you *want* to start, or when it can be done most easily and quickly. You have probably read of the studies made with identical twins, one of whom was taught with patience and difficulty to climb stairs at a very early age, while the other was left to pursue his own infant inclinations. The outcome, of course, was that when he was ready to climb stairs, the untrained twin learned the trick quite easily, and was soon nearly as proficient as his carefully trained brother. You will find that the results will be much the same with dogs.

Yes, you can train a pup while he is still quite young. And what he learns then will stay with him longer than if you wait until he is older to begin to work with him. But there are also other questions to early training—just how serious, you will have to decide for yourself. Will you perhaps expect too rapid progress from the puppy? Would he perhaps respond a good deal more quickly if he were a little older and had established more rapport with you? Is the extra patience and effort required to train a very young pup really worth it to you?

I can only tell you what I have learned by training hundreds of dogs: I personally prefer that a dog be at least eight months old before I begin serious training work. (Housebreaking, of course, is accomplished much earlier.) I have found that the average dog's capacity to learn continues to increase for a considerable span of time. I can achieve more rapid results with a dog that is two years old than with one that is only eight months old.

Another question you will be asking is: Must the dog receive reinforcement every time he responds properly? The answer is *No*. For the first fifteen or twenty proper reactions to the signal, you should by all means give him his reinforcing bite. But after that, if you occasionally skip the tidbit, it will do no harm. He won't quit the course.

You will also want to know how long you have to keep up this business of providing tidbits as reinforcements. Your first session should run to about forty trials, and most of the correct responses should have a happy tidbit ending. The second session will have fewer trials, and after that, it shouldn't be necessary to use the reinforcement more than one time in five or six. Thereafter the patterns of behavior will be well established. Voice control, showing your pleasure and rapport, will be all the inducement you need.

Dogs, as I keep saying, are not people. But they are almost as individual and almost as unpredictable. How many times do you suppose your parents had to remind you to say thank you, or to shake hands properly, or to stand up when an older person came into the room? It's the same with your pup. You keep on teaching him until he learns what he should know. Then you stop. But he remembers.

Brushing as a Reinforcement

We've already made the point that dogs like to be scratched instead of petted. Many dogs are also delighted with a good brushing. If your dog feels that way, his brush may be a handy reinforcement, one you can use to replace or supplement food in special cases.

My Old Blue, a coon dog I once owned, loved to be brushed. I used a 25-cent scrub brush and brushed hard. He couldn't get enough. And because of that, he learned to respond to the signals "chair" and "table," to jump onto the table where I regularly brushed him.

49

A collar is easy, but a leash sometimes makes trouble. Phoebe learned by dragging a chain along the ground.

It was easy to train him. I brushed him when he was lying down. Then I held the brush above him. He stood up, to be near the brush. I put him on the table and groomed him there, and then I put him back on the floor. When I held the brush over the chair beside the table, he immediately climbed onto the chair, and as he did, I said "chair" and brushed him. When I had finished, I tipped the chair so that he had to. jump down—and I said "down." I repeated the series—"chair," "down," "chair," "down,"—a good number of times, though he had learned to recognize "chair" as a signal within six repetitions.

I used the same method to teach him to jump from the chair to the table. A second session the next night fixed the signals and actions in his mind permanently.

Blue's companion in our house was Marble, a Cocker Spaniel who didn't like to be brushed. In fact, before he was trained, he had to be leashed to a post on the table when the job was done—and under those circumstances it *was* a job. With him I used food instead of a brush as reinforcement. I was able to teach him, too, to jump from floor to chair to table on signal. I always brushed Marble first, and Blue learned to sit in the chair, waiting his turn when Marble jumped down.

The moral of this, clearly, is that though food may be the most universal reinforcement, it is not the only one you can use.

Dogs or Seals?

You may still be asking, "Why reinforcements?" I suppose that you have heard or read as often as I have that a dog just loves to please you and doesn't need food as a reward. "Remember," some people will tell you vehemently, "your dog is no seal."

The truth may be that the seal is more intelligent than the dog. Has anyone ever made a comparison of the intelligence of the two? Has anyone ever seen a dog perform the truly phenomenal balancing acts which seals are capable of? Has anyone ever seen a dog trained to play a tune on horns as seals do? Seals are not beneath contempt. Not my contempt, anyway.

Seals are intelligent animals; they respond, as dogs do, to reinforcements. Watch the skillful trainer feed each seal a fish after each trick. Does he wait until the seal has completed his whole act and then feed him offstage? He doesn't. The instant the balanced ball is off the seal's nose, he is given his reinforcement, his fish.

Keep in mind a picture of that skillful animal-training when you are training your dog. If I could teach a dog to perform the way seals do and the dog wanted a fish—I'd give him a fish!

51

CHAPTER SEVEN

Your Dog's Abilities

You may be wondering what and how much your dog can be taught. Well, usually a good deal more than you expect.

You must realize, however, that what he learns and how quickly he learns depends on a fairly intricate complex of behavior patterns—and on how efficiently you use them for your purposes. You need not, as we've said, be a dog psychologist to succeed with your training program, but you should at least be aware of some of the factors involved.

All dogs learn. They have to. If you put a dog out alone in the woods, he will learn to get along somehow. His reflexes will help him to survive; so will his inherited behavior patterns. There are a multitude of these patterns, and you must remember that they manifest themselves in different ways, at different ages, even at different times of the year.

Glands, for example, play an important role. When the days get longer, and again when they become shorter, bitches come into heat and behave in their characteristic

52

Your dog's senses are keener than you think. They are all operating even when he seems to be just playing.

manner. The male dogs of the neighborhood are stimulated and they, too, behave in a manner different from their normal. You could say that the change in the length of day is thus responsible basically for the change in behavior. Or you could just as well say that glandular changes in the pituitary glands were responsible for the changes in the behavior of the neighborhood dogs.

Inherited patterns are also determining factors. Over the centuries we have altered the nature of various breeds of dogs by selection so as to make them more useful for certain jobs—sheep-herding, guarding, coursing, bird-hunting. Even within the last hundred years, dogs have been startlingly improved and specialized. Today we have several breeds of tree hounds. Pointing breeds have been bred to cover more ground at high speeds. Beagles hunt rabbits differently from the way other hounds follow them. Retrievers are most proficient in following their handler's guiding signs and in the ease with which they can be trained.

Because of these fixed inherited behavior patterns, some breeds learn certain tasks with much greater ease than do others. It is like mathematical ability, or musical ability, or mechanical skills in human beings, or the love of breeding animals to improve them. Some of us lack these talents while others possess them to a high degree.

Naturally, therefore, some dogs learn some lessons more quickly than others. Nevertheless, most of the useful tricks and tasks can be taught to almost any dog of any breed. And all dogs, no matter of what breed, learn the same way: by what is to them trial and error.

A healthy, normal dog tries many things. Some turn out to be good for him, some bad. When he tries and something good immediately happens, he doesn't hesitate to repeat the action again and again, until it becomes habit. If he tries and something bad happens to him, he isn't likely to repeat it. Not often, at any rate. All his life, he tries and succeeds, he tries and fails.

In training, your job is to make the dog try. Reinforcements for behavior which pleases set the pattern for the habits you are trying to develop. Negative reinforcements extinguish behavior you do not want.

What makes this task relatively easy when you use the natural training method is that you can utilize the dog's ability to discriminate, an ability that is astonishingly broad and acute. A dog learns to react differently to different degrees of sound, to various odors, to distinctive shapes—and does so very readily. To him each person he encounters has a special, distinct odor. Each one looks different. Any dog can distinguish his master from a stranger at a considerable distance. And, as in the example mentioned earlier, some even learn to identify a car by sounds that are totally inaudible to human beings.

Dogs learn by trial and error. Phoebe isn't certain whether what she sniffs ahead is good or bad.

Most people are astonished to learn how accurately and well dogs can discriminate. It has been demonstrated, for instance, that a dog can determine the origin of a distant sound to within five degrees of the 360 degrees in a circle. Think of the discrimination a Bloodhound exhibits when he picks out and follows one man's trail across ground where perhaps a hundred others have walked. Or of the coon hound I once knew who, for some reason, chose to trail only mature male raccoons. During one entire hunting season he did not tree a single young or female animal.

What you need to remember is that your dog has the ability to learn more things faster than you expect—*if* you encourage him to try, reinforce his successful attempts in his trial and error method, and fully utilize his remarkable sense perceptions.

CHAPTER EIGHT

The Workshop

From here on you will see a great deal more of Maggie and Phoebe and hear much less from me. All I want to do here is tell you a bit about the way Phoebe's education was handled.

You will see that most of her training sessions were conducted on a table. I make no apologies for that old kitchen table. It is like any other except that it was raised to a height of 36 inches instead of the usual 30. That was done simply to make things easier for Maggie and for the photographer. It was also covered with a taut, rough cloth so that Phoebe was confident of her footing.

I suggest that you train your dog on a similar raised platform. You can get the same results working with the dog on the floor. But that will mean that you will either have to sit on the floor, too, or spend a good part of the session stooping and bending. If you can find an old table of the right size which you can push up against a wall somewhere, the lessons will go easier for you.

In the wall above the table you will notice a hook, or eye bolt. It should be put in at about the height of your

Phoebe went to class on this table. She soon learned to like it, waited patiently for the lesson to begin.

dog's back when he is standing on the table. The dog's leash is fastened to it so that he can move around freely as far as the edge of the table, but is prevented from hopping off in pursuit of the tasty reinforcements in your pocket.

It is likely that your pupil is also used to the collar and leash. On the chance that he isn't, however, we might digress for a moment to discuss ways of acquainting him with this new experience.

Phoebe had been trained to her collar and leash before her formal training sessions began. This was helpful especially because a leash to Phoebe means fun. When she sees it in Maggie's hand, she's immediately excited and pleased. And she will follow the leash, almost dancing all the way from her kennel to the training room. That's a good way to begin a training session.

You have one advantage if you must do the collar and leash training now. You won't have to overcome any dislike of leashes—the result of force training which "broke" the dog to the leash. And you can make sure your dog is as delighted to see his leash as Phoebe is.

The collar is no problem at all. Just buy one that will be slightly tight, so your pup can't possibly slip it over his head. No, it won't hurt him. In fact, most dogs behave as if they didn't realize they had on collars.

The leash, however, will probably not be accepted so willingly. One common method for accustoming a dog to it is simply to fasten it to his collar and tie the other end to a tree or post. He'll fight it until he realizes he can't win. After a while his resentment fades. He becomes resigned to the leash.

But you *can* teach your dog to accept the leash with pleasure. My Bloodhounds, for instance, associated both their leashes and their harnesses with their favorite activity, man-trailing. At the sight of the harnesses they jumped with excitement or crowded around the doors of their kennel runs. Your pup probably has simpler pleasures than manhunts, but you can see to it that he's just as delighted when you show him his leash.

First, attach the leash to his collar when you're taking him for a walk. Don't hold the leash. Just let him drag it along as the two of you go on your way. After a few days, use a chain or a heavier leash for your next two or three walks. This won't faze him, either.

Now, choose a time when your dog is hungry. Take him for a walk and carry along some tidbits of food in your pocket. Take hold of his leash. Be firm. When he holds back, say "heel" and when he does (that is, when he is along your right side), give him a tidbit. Walk farther. Each time he holds back, say "heel." And each time he arrives at your side, reinforce that action with a tidbit. Two days, at thirty repetitions each, should see your pup heeling. He will be leash-trained, and the two of you can get on to other lessons.

Phoebe's preliminary training included two other lessons. You may prefer *not* to teach them to your pup unless he is of a breed which needs constant grooming—a Poodle, a modern Cocker, a Wire Haired Terrier, or an Afghan Hound, for example.

We knew much of Phoebe's training would happen on the table. So, first, she was taught to jump on a chair, then to jump on the table. These lessons took her eleven and nine minutes respectively. After that she reacted immediately to the signals, and took herself to the table for each lesson.

You can judge the timing of most of Phoebe's training sessions, by the way, by keeping an eye on the clock in the pictures.

The Effect of a Change of Environment

Phoebe was a raw, kennel dog. She had never seen the inside of a house until after her training sessions. When

59

she was brought into our home, she was insatiably curious about everything in the room. We had to keep her on her leash for a time to prevent her rushing to investigate each new, strange thing she saw. And she seemed to forget some of her lessons.

It took almost as long as a normal training session to get Phoebe to pay attention properly. However, with the aid of the leash (for a while only) and a few repetitions of the things she had learned, she calmed down and her behavior became exemplary.

The first lesson was to jump from floor to chair to training table. Phoebe was a little slow: Time—20 minutes.

For some reason the pupil didn't seem to trust that chair. Maybe it was because it wobbled a little.

Your pup is probably used to your house already. But if he's been trained somewhere else—in the garage or basement, for example—he will have to get used to doing his tricks in the house. Indeed, if he's trained in one room, you may have to have a short refresher session to get him to perform in other rooms.

Don't be discouraged. This is normal and expected behavior. Just put your pup through his various paces again, and he'll soon respond in his new environment. In many of the lessons which follow, you'll find some notes on continuing the training in new places.

But it's time now for *you* and *your* dog to go to work.

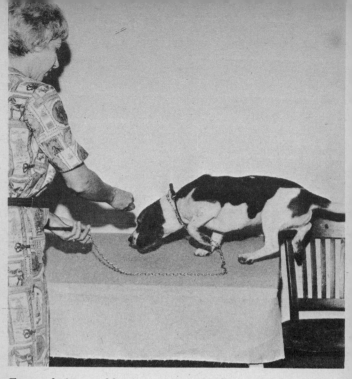

From chair to table was easier. Phoebe is still a bit uncertain here, but she soon grew accustomed to the height.

TO SHAKE HANDS

This isn't a particularly useful trick, but it's a good one to try first.

Some dogs seem to react to "shake hands" almost automatically. They need only the friendly pressure of a hand around a paw, or to feel you pump it up and down, or perhaps a good scratch at the base of the ear with your other hand for encouragement. It's one trick that seems to work all right with the love-to-please method, and it *can* be taught that way.

She has it now. The idea is to shake hands with the teacher, not to pat her.

Phoebe was used to her kennel and the living room was strange. But a well-learned lesson is remembered any-where.

65

hook his chin over his food dish as you are setting it down on the floor, and then you'll have a mess to clean up. A session or two in the workshop will prevent this nuisance forever.

Your dog's safety is perhaps a more important consideration. If you live in the suburbs, there is a good chance that some time when you are out for an evening stroll, your dog will encounter a slow-moving black pussy with white stripes. If he rushes at it, command "don't touch!" sharply. Unhappily, the warning is likely to come too late, and by the time he hears you, he will catch that powerfully acrid skunk odor and feel an intense burning in his eyes—a negative reinforcement that your dog will probably remember for the rest of his life.

Teacher is being firm here. The tidbit is really too small and too tasty to resist.

(Incidentally, if that should happen to him, he is going to be almost impossible to live with for a while. The best way I have ever discovered to get rid of the odor is—believe it or not—to give him a good bath in a gallon or so of tomato juice, and follow this with a good sudsing. It works. I don't know quite why, but it does.)

If you vacation in some northern parts of the country, your dog could learn an even worse lesson should he be tempted to tangle with a porcupine, unless you shout "don't touch" just before he attacks. Some persons think that pulling the quills will teach him a lesson, but actually it has almost no such effect. Why? Because the pain caused by pulling quills—and it is a severe pain—is too long removed from the quilling for your dog to connect it as a lesson.

Phoebe succumbs. Maggie, being a good teacher, does what has to be done, but not quite emphatically enough.

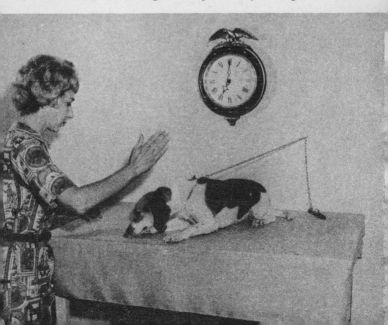

Teacher explains it all over again, and apparently the pupil understands and agrees.

All the lesson he gets out of a quilling is the pain inflicted at the moment of biting and for a short time afterward because the memory is kept alive by the lasting pain. By the time you get him to a veterinarian or get out your car pliers and pull quills, the lag between cause and effect is too great. And in this there is a lesson for us which it does no harm to reiterate: The reinforcement, negative or positive, must be almost part of the action to provide a lesson.

Teach your dog "don't touch." It is one of the most useful and important lessons he can learn.

How It's Done

In training, use a large-sized dog biscuit or a knuckle

The idea, it seems, is to ignore that tasty morsel, no matter how delicious it smells.

bone—anything good to eat but too big to be picked up and swallowed in a hurry. The session can be conducted on the table or the floor, or first on the table and then the floor.

Drop the food in front of your dog. Say "don't touch!" sharply. He will grab it, however. *As he does,* slap him beside the cheek. If he doesn't drop the object instantly, you didn't slap hard enough. Father says to little Willie before he spanks him, "Son, this is going to hurt me more than it does you." In this case, your slap really *should* hurt you more than it does your dog. That is, unless he's a midget dog. Even then, a good sharp slap will frighten more than hurt him.

Repeat as many times as necessary until your pupil stands back from the object when you command "don't touch."

This is negative reinforcement. It's less pleasant than using tidbits. But remember, it is for his own good and safety.

TAKE IT

After your dog has learned the meaning of "don't touch," you should start teaching him "take it." In fact, both lessons could be part of the same session, but to avoid the chance of confusing the dog, it is safer to teach him the two in separate lessons.

How It's Done

Training is a simple matter of allowing him to have the object he's learned to avoid at the command "don't touch." As you give it to him or let him pick it up, say "take it." He will, of course, but you won't be sure that he has learned the lesson until he responds properly to both the "don't touch" and "take it" signals as you give them. Repeat until you are sure he understands.

You may wish to use other signals. I've taught some of my dogs not to touch when I say "wait" and that it was all right to touch when I said "now." The signals, of course, don't matter so long as you always use the *same* signals.

When your pupil has learned to obey "don't touch" and "take it" in his usual training place, take him to a different part of the house, and be sure he responds properly to the words there. Have other members of your family give the signals.

It is also useful to take him outside on a long training cord where you know there will be a distraction, say a cat. If he runs at the cat, call "don't touch" and upend him if he doesn't stop. You will often have to repeat this several times, and to do it properly, you will need the

70

This early in the lesson there are sure to be mistakes, consequences, and (below) reconciliations.

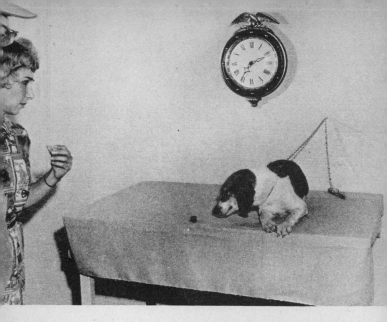

Phoebe looks, yearns, and sniffs—and is congratulated when she obeys the command "Don't touch."

cooperation of a strong-minded cat. I hope you have one in your neighborhood.

Every time you feed him, say "don't touch" and make the dog wait until his food dish is in its proper place. Then say "take it." There are few easier reactions to condition a dog to than these, and few more useful.

TO COME

Dogs can be taught to come to you on command in several ways. The simplest way, I've found, is to use *two* teachers stationed some distance apart.

In our kennels, one person stands inside, the other outside at the end of the run. In his training session, the dog has to race the length of the kennel run, receive his reinforcement from the person who called him there, then race back through his entrance and across his room to receive another from the assistant who has summoned him at that end.

Another successful method I have used is to attach a twenty-foot training cord to a fence or a stake in the ground. One teacher stands twenty feet from the stake on one side, the other the same distance from it in the opposite direction.

You can also carry out the training in an apartment, with the two teachers in different rooms.

Wherever the session is held, the procedure is the same.

How It's Done

Your dog is comfortably hungry. One of the teachers says "come!" When the pup wanders closer to the person, he'll smell the reinforcement and is given it as the word "come" is repeated. He wanders away again. The same teacher again says "come." When he goes to the sound —it should be repeated again distinctly—he's again given a tidbit. He'll soon learn the signal.

Phoebe learned to come on command almost immediately —before the appearance of that small, dark man.

You'll squat down to give the tidbit, but I've found that it's a good idea to stand up after each trial. This encourages the dog to wander away to explore his surroundings. Otherwise he will stay beside you, and the lesson will be slowed down.

Now it's time for the second teacher to go to work. He, too, calls "come!" The dog will hear and go to investigate. And there, to his delight, he receives another tidbit. From this point on, he should catch on to things in a hurry.

Repeat until you can count twenty correct reactions, ten each from the two teachers.

After these twenty trials, the pup will probably begin to run to the two teachers alternately. He has a tidbit, then he hears the signal, and he expects to go to the other person. You must extinguish this automatic pattern of response. Wait until he has run halfway or more to the other teacher. Then call him back to you. If he goes on to the other teacher, he gets, of course, no reinforcement. For a few trials he may seem confused. He'll catch on again, however, within fifteen minutes.

Twenty more trials in each direction should fix the pattern. Make sure that he remembers by reviewing the lesson again at another training session.

Learning "Come" Away from Home

This is the important lesson, for it makes certain, or should, that your dog will always heed your call.

Take your pup for a walk, and take along the training cord. Fasten the cord to his collar. As you walk along, he'll start to run for a familiar tree or perhaps another dog. Call "come." If he doesn't heed your call, hold fast to the cord and upend him when he reaches the end of it. *Don't* pull him to you! If you do, you will merely be reverting to the old force method.

Make more tries, and when he does come at your call,

give him a tidbit. This process may take many lessons unless you know a place to walk him—in a park, for example—where there are plenty of distractions.

It's a natural reaction for you to scold your pup when he doesn't come to you on command. But don't do it. Give him a tidbit when he *does* come. The upsetting when the cord stops him short is all the scolding he needs. Any cross words or other discipline will simply make him not want to return to you, and that cancels out his earlier lesson.

TO SIT

This is as easy as any lesson you will ever teach. In

Back to the training table for an easy lesson. The pupil has learned to sit almost before the clock has started.

If you use the natural method, you will have no difficulty in teaching your dog to stand or to lie.

fact, you have already learned one method to teach your dog to sit (Chapter 6). Here is a way that is even·less trouble.

How It's Done

Your pup is comfortably hungry and *standing* on the table. Take a tidbit in your hand and move it toward him. Usually he will sit down promptly. Sometimes, however, he may back up. If he does, draw him forward and repeat your action with the tidbit. As he sits, say "sit." Give him the tidbit. *Don't* push his rear down! We want voluntary action, not forced. Reinforcements alone will condition your pup to sitting at the signal "sit." After that, sitting on command, but without reinforcement, will be automatic.

Repeat thirty or forty times during the first lesson—about ten minutes—twenty times during a second lesson, and you should have a dog that will sit down promptly whenever you tell him to.

TO STAND AND TO LIE DOWN

"Stand" is a most useful command for your pup to know. It gets him up if you want to move the throw-rug he is lying on, and makes it considerably easier to nudge him over if he has chosen your seat in the car.

"Lie down" is equally important. It can prevent a host of annoyances—from your dog's pawing you to attract your attention when you want to read a book to his making an absolute nuisance of himself when he joins you in greeting your guests.

Now, I've been told by dog-trainers of the old school that a dog will learn only *one* command at a time. In any session, they will tell you, you can either teach him to "stand" or you can teach him to "lie down." But if you try to do both, many trainers contend, you will confuse and confound him.

It is true, I think, that it is a mistake to try to teach a dog two unrelated responses at the same time. But when they *are* related—as they are in the case of "stand" and "lie down"—I think that you are actually wasting time if you *don't* teach them at the same time. Dogs, I have always found, are remarkably quick to learn alternate actions such as these. Maggie taught Phoebe to respond properly in a single session. I have done the same thing with dozens of dogs, and I don't doubt that you can do it with yours.

How It's Done

Begin with your pup lying down. Hold a tidbit above him. He'll stand up to try and get it. As soon as he is on

78

all fours, say "stand," and give him the tidbit. Now tell him "lie down." If he does, give him another reinforcement. If he doesn't, don't push him down. Simply hold your hand with the tidbit low; when the dog flops down to get it, say "lie down," and give him the food. As soon as he has swallowed it, hold another tidbit well above him and say "stand."

Before you have repeated the up-down exercises a dozen times, you should find your pupil has learned to alternate. He'll take one tidbit standing up, then stretch out, ready for another, before you have a chance to say "lie down." That isn't what you want. You are training

The method is absurdly simple. It takes a little time, however, to learn the signals.

To lie and to stand—a simple alternating response learned
in a little less than the full 15-minute session.

him to respond to either signal, not both in automatic sequence. So give him the commands in various sequences. Now you give him his reinforcement *only* when he reacts properly to each signal. I expect that you will be able to break the alternating patterns in less time than it takes to tell you about the way it is done—and in one session you will have taught your dog two useful responses.

Here again, as with all of the tricks learned on the table, it's best to polish up his training in a different environment. Take your dog to the living room. Go through the repetitions again there. And, once again, don't stop too soon. Repeat until it becomes tiresome to you. There aren't any short cuts. The natural training method *itself* is the short cut.

TO ROLL OVER

This is an easy one—if you've already taught your dog "lie down."

How It's Done

Tell your dog "lie down." Now take a tidbit and hold to one side. He will reach for it. Let him keep his nose close to your hand and to the tidbit, but move them so that he has to turn his head. Eventually his body will have to turn, too. As his body comes over, say your signal word "roll." Give him the reinforcement as his legs touch the ground and he is lying on his other side. You then can have him turn back again or have him get up and lie down again—always so that he rolls over in the *same direction* each time.

When he has become well conditioned to having the reinforcement near his nose, try holding your hand farther and farther away. When this works well, put him on the floor and try standing over him.

81

For a good "roll over" lesson, you need more than table space. A rug will do, but a lawn is better

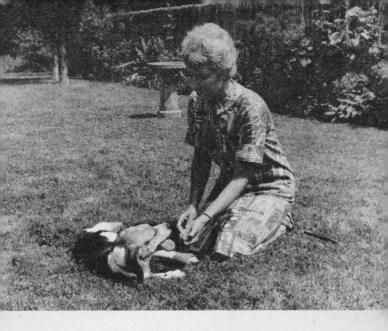

A simple circular motion is the basis of the whole lesson.
These four pictures tell the story.

Repeat about thirty times the first lesson; twenty the second.

The final tests, of course, come when he has learned to perform well outside the workshop. Try "roll over" in different places, and have other members of the family or people he knows well give the signal.

TO GO TO BED

Getting a dog into his sleeping place is often as much of a problem as getting a child to bed. Both dog and child are all too often shooed off to bed as a punishment. The kids have their own complicated reasons for wanting to stay up. Dogs sometimes have better reasons. Too many of them have uncomfortable beds, often of the corner-of-the-cellar variety with a rich crop of newly hatched fleas.

If your dog is to learn to run and jump into his box or bed without hesitation at your command, you should at least provide an inviting and comfortable place for him. It ought to be a good bed, one in which he can enjoy resting. It needn't be fancy or expensive. But it should, first of all, be big enough to allow him to sleep comfortably. It should have some sort of padding or nesting material which can be cleaned or changed from time to time. It should be in a place he can learn to like, not in some cold corner where he feels banished.

If the bed is right, training him to go to it will not be difficult.

How It's Done

The problem here is to find a way to teach your dog to go to bed *willingly* instead of being dumped there or driven there. The first thing to learn is not to *force* your dog to bed so that he thinks of it as a punishment or as the last safe place where he can escape your scolding. That's the usual motivation, but we're going to arrange things so that he *wants* to go there.

84

With the bed on the floor, going to bed was too easy.
When it was on the suitcase, we got our least flattering
picture.

It may look makeshift to you, but Phoebe likes her bed, goes there happily at bedtime.

The signal word is *"bed"*—and emphasize the *d* at the end, especially if your dog has already been taught *"beg."* Sometimes it's just as well to use the phrase "go to bed" to avoid confusion.

The routine is simple. Take your comfortably hungry dog to the bed. Hold a tidbit over it and, as he jumps onto the bed to get it, say "bed." Call him out again. Repeat this twenty times. Then say "bed," but don't hold the tidbit over it. If he jumps in anyway, then give him a tidbit.

Fifteen or twenty repeats should fix the pattern.

It is best, of course, to arrange to have this training session at the regular bedtime. But if it has been held earlier, when it's done, don't feed your dog the rest of his meal. Wait until his proper bedtime. Take his dish with his dinner in it, and walk to his bed. Say "bed," and when he is on the bed, give him his dinner right there.

Each night you'll repeat the signal "bed"—and at other times when you want your pup in his box. Probably he'll not need any more training than that. Most dogs don't. Saying "lie down" as soon as he's on the bed will help to make him stay put once he is there.

TO RECOGNIZE THE NAMES
OF DIFFERENT OBJECTS

The best way I've found to teach a dog the names of common household articles is to associate them with the *retrieving* which we discussed in the chapter, USING REINFORCEMENTS. In fact, you can consider the name-of-object lesson a kind of postgraduate exercise to "fetch."

How It's Done

Let's assume that your dog doesn't have the same peculiar aversion to a ball that Phoebe had. So you begin by training him during the first session to fetch the ball and drop it at your feet—and every time you throw the ball you say "fetch the ball." Your dog will then learn not only the meaning of "fetch" but he will also recognize the word "ball."

But you have to go a few steps further before he will be able to separate the command from the name of the object to be returned to you. If, at the next lesson you use an old shoe instead of a ball, and each time order him to "fetch the shoe," he will do that for you too. Now you throw first the ball and then the shoe, using the appropriate signal.

Next you toss both and say "fetch ball." He will be confused at first. If he retrieves the shoe, just turn your back on him and show displeasure. Turn and say "no, fetch ball." This will start him retrieving again, and he will soon learn that it is important to make the right choice and not simply return the first object he encounters.

If you have taught him "don't touch," you can use that signal very effectively if you see that he is about to make a wrong choice, and thus hasten his learning the name of different objects.

When you are certain that your dog has thoroughly learned the names of these first two objects, you can begin to substitute toys, the dog's leash or harness. When he knows the names of several things, you can tell him to fetch the one you want, and he will go about most industriously searching it out for you. You will be surprised how soon he will be pulling his leash off its hook to let you know he wants to go for a walk.

Associations of this kind develop quite rapidly. In the early 1900's there was a famous man-trailing Bloodhound called Nick Carter. His exploits were so extraordinary that his owner was often called from distant places to help find escaped convicts, or children who had strayed from home, or campers lost in remote areas. So often, in fact, that Nick learned to recognize the long ring of the old-fashioned telephone that meant a long distance call. He paid no attention at all to the usual sound of the phone, but when he heard that long ring, he invariably went to the wall, got his harness, and brought it to his owner. He was always willing to go.

I know a woman who is partially deaf. Her hearing seems to be selectively impaired. She can converse well enough on the phone, but, strangely, she cannot hear the bell unless she happens to be right beside it. So she has trained her dog to let her know when the phone rings.

We once had a Cocker whose recognition vocabulary included a remarkably long list of objects—including "kitten." Until the kitten was more than half grown, the dog on command would rush around and bring her back if she had hidden in a closet or strayed too far away on the lawn. Surprisingly, the cat seemed to enjoy being carried around in this unconventional way.

What you can teach your dog depends mostly on the time and patience you have. But you can be sure that he wants to learn and likes to learn. He is happy to fetch and carry for you.

TO CARRY

Carrying is simply an extension of retrieving. In that case your dog picks up the object you throw when you

Phoebe was not especially interested in retrieving things that Maggie tossed to the other end of the run.

But after she understood the game, she became an active and enthusiastic participant.

say "fetch" and brings it to you, drops it at your feet, and receives his reinforcement often enough to be conditioned.

How It's Done

To train your dog to carry after he has learned to fetch is a simple matter. When he comes to you, back away a short distance and say "carry" or whatever signal word you have chosen. Your dog will follow you. As you take the object he is carrying, reinforce him. Do this over and over, walking sideways at first and then in the usual way with your dog at your side. Each time you walk, make the distance longer and longer before you take the retrieved object and give him his reinforcement. At your first session you will probably be able to get your dog to carry an object 100 yards. At later sessions you can teach him little refinements such as how to hold objects in certain ways so as not to damage them.

For example, Phoebe was taught to carry a little Easter basket by its handle. At first she picked it up by its side, but she soon learned that holding the handle was the proper way; she received reinforcements only when she picked it up correctly. I suggest that if you want your dog to carry a basket, you begin with a small one and gradually use larger baskets. Be sure the handles are of a convenient size for the dog.

You begin the "carry" as a kind of add-on to retrieving. But you won't, of course, continue to toss the object you want the dog to carry. Simply pointing to it will be sufficient. Say "carry basket." If you have conditioned him to know "basket," you can then educate him to know the name of different objects—a paper bag, for example, with the top rolled down to give him something to grip. When he has practiced carrying first one and then the other, put both down together and say "carry bag." If he picks up the basket, say "no, bag." He will soon differentiate.

91

Strange to find a newspaper in the run—but there it was, and here she comes to the signal "Fetch."

But that, of course, gets us back to ways to teach your dog to recognize the names of objects—and that we have already done.

TO BEG

When I was a boy, as I remember, almost all little dogs were taught to sit up and beg. It was a simple parlor trick, harmless, amusing, and useless. But it was easy to teach even with the old methods, and so it was probably the most common accomplishment in the canine world.

Phoebe became an expert and appealing beggar in a matter of minutes.

How It's Done

Phoebe was trained on the table as usual, largely for Maggie's convenience. Besides, we reasoned that if Phoebe learned to sit up on the higher level, she would respond even better when she was on the floor, and indeed that turned out to be true.

The signal was "beg." The leash was fastened at the usual length and a tidbit was held at some distance above her head. As she stretched for it, the food was moved higher and backward so that she had to sit straight up to reach it. When she was in the proper position, Maggie said, "beg," and gave her the tidbit. Phoebe was allowed to drop back into the sitting position to savor the bite, and then the exercise was repeated. Phoebe learned what was expected after a dozen trials, but Maggie wisely continued the lesson through another 20 repetitions, by which time her student would instantly assume the begging position at the signal "beg."

Some dogs at first feel insecure when they sit up, and it may take them a little time to get over their fear. The temptation is to use a hand to steady them. But that is a mistake that will only delay the dog's progress. Don't help

93

him. Let him learn to respond voluntarily and to hold the position without any support from you.

Repeat the lesson at least 30 times during the first session and as many times again in the review period.

TO CATCH

Some dogs, particularly the Terriers, easily learn to catch objects in the air. And some don't. Phoebe, it turned out, was one who didn't. She had a hard time with this trick.

How It's Done

The ability to catch thrown objects isn't one a dog has by instinct. He has to learn it. At first it seemed that Phoebe needed bifocals. She could see the object falling, but when it came close to her—a foot or so above her head—she seemed suddenly unable to follow it with her eyes. She just let it drop or bounce off her nose and then found it on the table, using her nose instead of her eyes. But we knew there was nothing wrong with her sight. She could tell the difference between various shapes of food bits in her dish quickly enough.

Your dog may start off better than that. If he doesn't, you can do as Maggie did with Phoebe. I suggested she tie a reinforcement to a string and lower it slowly past Phoebe's head. When she did this, Phoebe reared up and snatched the food from the string. Maggie began to lower the string faster and faster. If Phoebe let it go past her mouth, Maggie jerked the food away. It took a little time, but after a while Phoebe learned that if she didn't grab the food while she had the chance, it would get away.

Next Maggie let the food, still on a string, swing past Phoebe—high enough that Phoebe had to jump to catch it when it came near her. This helped educate her to snatch reinforcements out of the air. And each time she did it, Maggie said "catch."

Phoebe seemed to be a natural beggar. She learned the trick in a few minutes —and ended up looking strangely like a penguin.

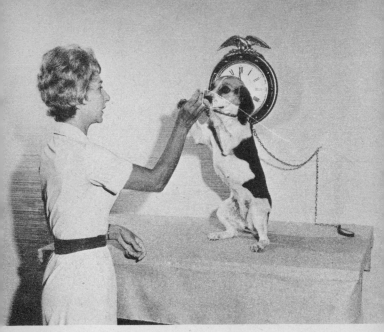

Like other girls, our student had some difficulties in learning how to catch things tossed to her.

But when she got the hang of the thing, she turned out to be a minor-league expert.

We used small pieces of boiled liver for this training. It's easy to thread a string near the edge of one and a slight pull at the liver breaks it away from the string which can then be re-threaded with another reinforcement.

When Phoebe had mastered catching tidbits on the string, Maggie began tossing them again—as slowly as she could, still saying "catch" each time. Those that Phoebe caught were hers. Those that she missed Maggie retrieved. Phoebe learned to catch.

It is true that it took three lessons for Phoebe to perfect her catching technique, but by the first five minutes of the second training session, she was able to catch anything that came within six inches of her nose. A third session turned her into a minor-league expert.

In these training sessions we followed the "catch" lessons with training Phoebe to "bed," then to "beg" and to "catch" her reinforcements. Next she learned to "sit" and "catch." At that third session she was able to perform them all. What impressed us most was that when we moved to the living room, Phoebe really shone. Not a miss; not a spot on the rug.

TO CLIMB A LADDER

I can't think of any really useful purpose for his accomplishment other than amusement.

It reminds me of a friend of mine who used to pleasure himself occasionally when he and his wife were sitting with friends on the terrace by asking, "Where's old Fido?" Nobody had seen a dog about the place, so my friend would set up a shrill whistling. In due time an enormous pet cat (called Fido) would come rushing up to get some morsel of reinforcement.

It made amusing small talk—and the story demonstrates again that signals are what you make them.

There's another reason to include this trick: to indicate to you that the natural training method will work even when you are teaching your dog something that he would ordinarily refuse to do. Dogs, as a rule, aren't climbers.

But before you try this one, you should be warned. If you keep your dog in a wire pen, you can expect him to be quite adept at climbing out after this course.

How It's Done

All the equipment you need to begin with is a four- or five-foot stepladder which you should lean against a table so that it will not be too steep. Your reinforcement can

Dogs are not climbers, and Phoebe quite evidently does not think that ladders were made for her.

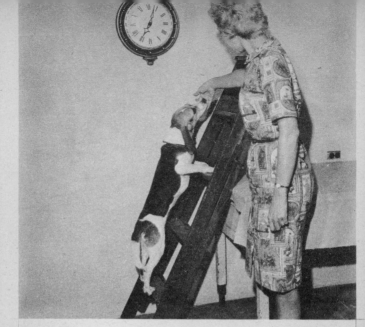

One step up isn't so bad—but the second step begins to look dangerous.

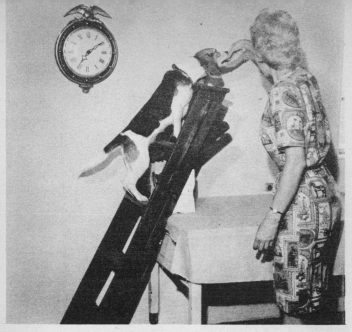

Phoebe makes the third step with the reinforcement at nose-tip—and is amazed at her own bravery.

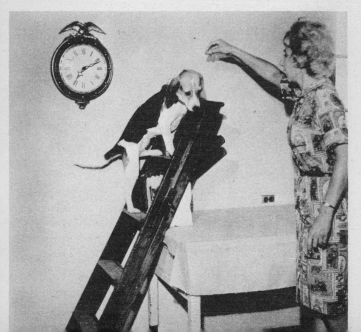

In one 15-minute session it is possible to get to the top of the ladder—and as high as Maggie can reach.

She wins teacher's approval in the classroom—and back at the kennel absolutely astounds her friends.

be kept on the table. Any word will serve as a signal—"climb," for example. In Phoebe's case, we used the word "fire," because it seemed cute. Now we can call "fire," and our little fire lassie climbs right up the ladder.

You must take one important precaution. Be sure the ladder will not slip. You can tack a piece of rubber to the bottom of the legs, or you can use some adhesive tape to attach the ladder firmly to the floor. But be certain it is dependably fixed in place. If it moves even once, the training time will be materially increased.

When your dog is 36-hours-hungry, call him over in front of the ladder. Hold the tidbit just high enough above your pupil's head so that he cannot reach it and then inch it upward as he attempts to get to it. Say "fire!" when he is extended upward as far as he can reach, and then give him the food. After he gets down, show him another tidbit and coax him in front of the ladder again. Then say "fire!" As he strains upward toward the reinforcement, repeat the word and give him his food.

Do this about ten times, and as he is learning to associate the word and the ladder, make him reach higher each time. He will step up with one hind leg and stretch toward the tidbit. When he gets both hind feet up on the first step, say "fire!" and give him the food. Then let him jump down.

As he gets more accustomed to the ladder and the height, coax him up another step, and reinforce when he makes progress.

At the second or third step your pupil will probably loose confidence and turn to jump down. However, the memory of the tidbits that are achieved at the end of the climb will soon start him up again. In Phoebe's case, after the first six times, which got her up on the first step, another eight trials were necessary to have her climb until her hind feet were on the third step. However, by that time she was conditioned enough so that she would run to

104

the foot of the ladder and start climbing at the word "fire!"

Step by step her confidence increased. Finally she would climb to the top, and sit reaching for her reinforcement.

Next, Maggie stood aside. A tidbit was placed on the top of the ladder where Phoebe could see it sticking over the edge. At the word "fire!" she would rush over and climb up the ladder and get it.

All of this transpired in fifteen minutes. Thereafter we repeated the climbing twenty times (about three times a minute) until Phoebe seemed solidly conditioned.

On a later trial, Phoebe did not behave so well in the living room. Just to see what would happen, we moved the retraining class outside. We set the ladder against the side of our home, under a window so the ladder top was even with the window sill. With a leash on our pupil, we got her climbing again at the word "fire!" After a few trials, we removed the leash and at the word "fire!" Phoebe would climb the ladder just as she did in the workshop.

Then I pushed up the screen to see if she would go inside looking for her reinforcement. She did—right across the kitchen sink where Mrs. Whitney had lunch waiting. Phoebe got her most tasty reinforcement.

The one I got was negative.

TO BE A WATCHDOG

A famous—or notorious—burglar once said that the best insurance against burglary a home-owner could buy was an alert, barking dog. The man had made a long and relatively successful career of rifling homes—before the judges finally put an end to it. He knew the tricks of his trade, and one of them was never to enter a house where there was a dog. Any dog, large or small.

Most dogs will bark naturally when they hear an unfamiliar sound around the house or see somebody who seems to them to be an intruder. Sometimes too insistently. Once in a while you will get a dog who has been hushed so often and so firmly that all barking is forbidden. And now and then you may encounter one who has become so pampered and sluggish that he won't respond to any situation, however alarming it might appear to a normal dog. But even the lazy, do-nothing kind can be taught to react to potentially dangerous people and events. Indeed, it is usually a good deal easier to teach them to sound an alarm than it is to get them to be quiet when you want them to be.

You are working with nature to reinforce the dog's natural instincts. Even a very young pup will bark to warn the rest of the pack whenever he encounters anything that is strange to him.

You have watched a flock of pigeons in the park. You know that when one flies up in sudden alarm, the rest fly up too. Or perhaps you have seen one startled sheep race off—followed by the whole flock. Is that merely imitation? No, psychologists call it allellomimintic behavior—and it doesn't make the slightest difference whether you can pronounce it or not. You merely have to learn how to use it to train your pet to be a watch dog.

Take your dog into your quietest downstairs room late in the evening. Sit in a chair and let the dog explore the place until he is satisfied and lies down beside you. Then he is ready. You have arranged to have an accomplice outside—a friend or neighbor whom the dog doesn't know too well. At a signal from you, your accomplice will push up the window a few inches or jiggle the knob of the door as though he were trying to enter the house. Immediately you hear the sound, jump up. Act as startled as you can. If you are a reasonably good actor, your excitement will be communicated to your dog, and he will run with you to the source of the strange noise. Pet him and give him a tidbit.

Return to your chair. Relax. Suddenly there is another noise from a different window. You both jump and rush toward it. The dog again gets reinforcement for his help. Repeat the performance. Usually before you have chased away the make-believe intruder more than four or five times, the dog will bark and run to the sound before you can even get out of your chair. Reinforce his good response each time.

You probably won't want your accomplice to prowl around outside doing his part twenty or thirty times, so it is best to invite him to cooperate with you only long enough to make ten or twelve trials. Ask him to come for another session a few days later. And again, perhaps, the next week. Your dog will usually react properly at the end of the first evening.

But remember you're not merely teaching the dog to guard the place when you are with him. Have other members of the family run some of the training sessions. And be sure, especially at the beginning, that the dog gets approbation and a bit of reinforcement when he volunteers to do a bit of guarding on his own.

RUNNING THROUGH THE REPERTOIRE

When your pup has learned to respond easily to several signals, it's worthwhile running him through them to keep him in practice. Put him through his paces from start to finish, and then perhaps go over them again in reverse order. Your dog will learn quickly, but he may forget if you don't have some kind of brush-up session once in a while. This isn't an immediate danger, of course. Dogs' memories are long, and a well-conditioned dog won't "lose his memory" unless he goes several months without practice.

Maggie rehearses Phoebe on the table where she was trained. Phoebe comes to these sessions comfortably hungry, just as she did for her lessons. Being hungry, she sometimes wants to stand at the edge of the table—the nearest spot to Maggie and the food. If this happens, Maggie uses the training chain hooked to the wall until Phoebe calms down. In a matter of minutes our dog has had her review and is ready for something new.

WORKSHOP SUMMARY

There is nothing special about the series of little tricks that Maggie taught Phoebe. They were merely examples intended to demonstrate how much easier it is to train a dog by using his natural inclinations to lead him along than it is to force him to learn in ways that are strange to him. The purpose was not to show you how to teach any particular lesson to your dog. Instead, it was to teach you how to apply the training method in a variety of ways.

Once you understand the principles, you can apply them as you see fit.

One word of caution, however: Don't try to train your dog to do jobs that not natural to him. Individual breeds have special talents born into them. These special abilities vary greatly from breed to breed. It's a waste of time to give music lessons to a person with no musical talent. It's just as pointless to try to make a bird dog out of a hound, or a rabbit dog out of a Collie.

The exercises you see Phoebe doing here can be taught to any breed of dog, no matter what their inherited talents. We haven't discussed special training here. But it must be evident to you that such teaching can be done as well with the natural method. For each breed the kind of training differs. The basic method, however, remains the same.

One final admonition: I hope that just because this method of training seems easy, you won't be tempted to become what I call an "armchair trainer." Owners of this stripe have talents for sitting and dreaming. They are often ambitious, too, but they rarely succeed in training their dogs properly.

Results in dog training come from work. The natural method makes the work easier, quicker, and more pleasant. But teaching still demands time, repetition, enthusiasm, and patience. Your dog has all these qualities. The question, however, is how many of them do you have?

CHAPTER NINE

To Break Bad Habits

By now you certainly know the principle of conditioning. We've demonstrated the method with Phoebe in a dozen ways. You can train your dog to do scores of other things simply by using the same kind of reinforcement to establish good habits.

But it's just as important to stop bad habits. And reinforcements are the answer for that, too, another kind that we have already mentioned, *negative reinforcements*.

When you wanted to teach your dog to do something, you showed him what you wanted him to do, and then you reinforced the correct response by fulfilling a need— by giving him some food. You could, perhaps, if you had the time and patience, teach your dog *not* to do something simply by refusing to provide the reinforcement. But as we have said, to be most effective, the reinforcement must be instantly and directly connected with the act. Withholding the reinforcement doesn't have that instant effect. It is more likely to leave your dog puzzled and frustrated.

You will surely want to teach your dog *not* to do certain things, and to do that you have to turn the reinforce-

You appreciate affection, of course, but there are times when you can get too much of a good thing.

ment system inside out and use reinforcement in a different way.

Let's take a simple example. Your dog wants and needs affection. So he jumps up against you and you pet him, rub his ears, and generally give him the attention he craves. Naturally he'll jump up against you every chance he has. But you can get more of that than you need—especially when his paws are muddy and you're wearing a freshly pressed suit. And if he is really outgoing, your guests are going to be unpleasantly overwhelmed.

How do you handle this problem? I've owned a lot of big dogs, and a good many of them were excessively friendly. Though I've tried all sorts of methods to discourage pawing affection, I finally came back to two handy negative reinforcements. When one of my dogs jumps up against me, I don't push him down or scold him. I stroke his head and pet him. But I want him to discover that jumping up has unpleasant consequences. So, while I pet him, I also press my toe sharply on his hind feet—hard enough to hurt him. He doesn't see my foot—but he very quickly learns that though I obviously like him, something unpleasant happens when he jumps up against me.

If that seems too harsh, or if you object to having your foot and hand in such duplicitous disagreement, get a handshake buzzer from a trick store—one of those practical joker's gadgets that are wound up, hidden in the palm of a hand, and set to buzzing startlingly by the pressure of a handshake. Keep it in the palm of your hand. When your pup jumps on you, pet him. That, of course, will set off the buzzer. He won't like it a bit, especially if you run it close to his ear. And if it happens fairly regularly when he jumps up against you, he'll stop.

In my years in veterinary practice, I learned that the dyed-in-the-wool pet lover was often reluctant to use negative reinforcements. But if you have a dog, you ought to be willing to discipline him (in his way) just as you do your child. You needn't be distressed when you use these don't-do-it reinforcements. Your dog certainly won't be. For him the process is simple. He tries something, finds out that the consequences are bad, and therefore avoids it in the future. He associates the *action,* not you, with painful results.

Negative reinforcement is conditioning. That's not the same thing as punishment, a term which applies more properly to human beings. People have imagination and an ability to think into the future. They can visualize good and bad in terms of rewards and punishments. A dog has little if any of that ability. If he's to understand the consequences of any action, the bad or good results must happen almost as soon as the action itself.

When a dog touches a glowing ember, he feels instant pain. If, on the other hand, he saw the ember, touched it, and half a minute later felt the pain, the experience would be of little use in teaching him to avoid glowing embers.

Match your negative conditioning to the lesson of that glowing ember. Never threaten. Do something, or keep quiet. The only thing a dog can understand in a threat is the unfriendly tone of your voice. And he probably doesn't even understand the reason for that.

What methods will you use to condition your dog negatively? How harsh need they be to be effective? Let's go back again to nature. A little puppy learns very quickly what a growling sound means. He responds to his mother's growl itself. It doesn't mean one time, "Get away from the food dish or I'll nip you," and the next time, "Stop biting my ears." It just means "Bad!" and applies to whatever the puppy is doing at the moment the growl occurs.

The mother dog doesn't gentle her puppy along by tapping him lightly with her tail. She may bite him so hard that he bleeds. She may toss him against the side of a pen so that it hurts painfully and he screams in terror. Now, I'm not advising that you should be so harsh. I'm simply reminding you how the natural dog is taught.

Certainly you don't want to hurt your dog or frighten him unnecessarily. But you do want to train him, to teach him to behave properly. And one of the methods you will have to use from time to time is negative conditioning—and that means using his natural response to pain and fear.

That's the way he learns. He'll catch a toad once—and for the rest of his life he will remember that bitter, corrosive taste. Odors can also be actually painful to him. Sounds, too. He'll be frightened half out of his wits if he knocks a dish off the table and it smashes on the floor.

You aren't likely to use bad odors or foul tastes or crashing sounds to train your dog. Instead, you will use the same kind of deterrents his mother would use—stern enough to achieve your purpose, not so harsh as to injure him.

Usually these methods will be simple, obvious, and direct. You will, for example, learn to make proper use of the flat of your hand.

The Open Hand

Dogs learn that hands feed them, that they produce the things dogs like. And sometimes their actions show that the realization that this beneficent part of a human being can deal out a good sharp smack as well as dole out food comes as a real educational surprise. And a good one, too.

You may hear that your hand must represent kindness and nothing else to your pup. Don't believe it! Use your hands as situations demand.

When it's necessary, give your misbehaving pup a sharp smack beside the cheek. And I do mean *smack,* not tap. Except with tiny dogs, to be effective, a smack must make your hand sting. Your hand will hurt you more than the dog's cheek will hurt him.

You won't be unnecessarily rough with your dog, but sometimes a good smack is better than days of nagging.

The Rolled Newspaper

The rolled newspaper is effective, but only when used properly. It does have one special advantage. The sound it makes when you whack adds to the effect of the blow.

Roll up a newspaper and smack yourself across the thigh. It takes quite a hard whack to hurt much—and your dog's hide is less sensitive than yours. So use it with impressive and noisy vigor. I've seen dogs who were merely angered when struck glancingly with a newspaper, and stubborn ones who have even taken the paper away from the would-be trainer. A newspaper can't be very painful, so if you use one, make it sound bigger than it really is.

A rolled newspaper is a handy correctional device. It doesn't hurt much—but it makes a lot of noise.

A good shaking will impress any recalcitrant pup. And, properly done, it will blur any picture.

Shaking

This method, of course, can be used only on small dogs. But it's about the most effective of any negative reinforcement I've ever found. Just pick the miscreant up by the scruff of the neck and shake him. This treatment doesn't hurt him very much, and it shouldn't distress you. But it does scare the daylights out of the pup, and it will give him a healthy respect for you. I've used it to stop bullies from tormenting weaker dogs. A good sound shaking takes even the most recalcitrant pup down several pegs. Of course, it's a drastic measure. Save it for the worst kind of behavior.

This Hurts Me More . . .

I seem to have been urging you to "hit 'em harder" through most of this chapter. I know there are thousands of people who would rather read about a child being thrashed than a dog being whacked. And to them especially I must seem harsh. I can only remind them that nature itself is not always gentle. If you want your dog to learn to live in our overcrowded world, then you must provide the kind of conditioning he needs to live in it well.

The Need for Reconditioning

It's not easy to abolish a bad habit forever. Sometimes it will recur. When it does, you must be ready with the appropriate negative reinforcement.

Running instead of coming when he is called is one of those undesirable habits which reasserts itself periodically even with a well-trained dog. Your signal "come" begins to mean nothing. If you let things go, it may begin to look like the signal for "run away." More likely, there will be a confusion. "Come" may mean what it says inside the house, but outside it doesn't seem to apply. You can change your dog's mind about that in a few sessions of conditioning.

Take him walking with a long, light cord attached to his collar. He should be comfortably hungry, as always in these sessions. If he goes his own way when you say "come," pull back on the cord and upset him. If he comes on signal, give him a tidbit of food. The jerk of the cord and the sprawl which follows are negative reinforcements enough. You may have to go through this reconditioning from time to time. But at least you won't be in the spot of the Vermonter whose oxen ran away with him and his hay rack: He yelled "whoa" until he saw that it wouldn't work. Then, not to be defeated by dumb beasts, he switched to another command. "Giddap!" he said, "you *will* obey."

Let's take some of the common misbehavior problems that you are likely to encounter with your dog.

To Stop Barking

Every now and then you'll get a barking dog. He doesn't simply bark when there is something to bark about—a stranger on the walk, an unusual sound, a cat crossing the yard. He just barks. His noise bothers you, and it drive your neighbors to distraction. They call you, or the city fathers, to complain. What do you do?

There are at least two painless and effective ways to stop his barking.

If your dog lives in a doghouse in the back yard, you can use a vigorously direct method. Take him out of his house and close the door so that he can't get in. Then set a container of water on the ground where he can see it—half a bucket for a large dog, a quart for a small one.

The instant he barks, run outside, dash the water over him and say "quiet!" or "still!" Fill the container again and go inside the house. Rush out and slosh him whenever he barks. Go right on doing it until he has associated the dunkings with his barking. This method works. Almost always he'll stop his nuisance noise.

But it's important, once you start this training, not to let your dog get away with his barking at any time. No exceptions! When he barks, don't wait until he has stopped; start running toward him while he is still making the racket. When he's learned his lesson the first day, your training job won't be finished. You will have to repeat the sloshings until he's truly cured.

If you live in an apartment, however, you are not going to throw buckets of water around the living room. You'll use a neater method—the dark closet treatment. Shutting your pup alone in the darkness can be a most effective negative reinforcement. Your dog starts to bark—just to make a noise. You say "quiet!" He keeps on barking. So you snatch him up and dump him in a dark closet. He'll quiet down pretty quickly. Then you let him out. When he starts to bark again, back to the closet he goes. But about the time he begins to associate barking with the

118

closet—perhaps before—your dog will learn to run away from you to avoid being stuck in the dark. So attach a six-foot cord to his collar. You can catch him easily merely by stepping on the cord.

I can tell you this: A headstrong, spoiled dog is almost certain to be thoroughly disliked by everyone but his master. The fault is not his. It is his master's—for being too lazy to train his dog *not* to do things which are unnecessary, unpleasant, and disturbing.

The dark closet is the ultimate indignity. It's effective—if you have a strong arm and a small dog.

I remember how I once saved the life of a fine coon hound—and, I'm sorry to say, by applying negative reinforcing of a kind I wouldn't recommend or use today. He was called TNT. He was black and tan, had changed hands six times. I bought him from the pound for $5.00. He was an incorrigible barker. When I took him, he'd been already condemned to the gas chamber.

I tried the water method first. TNT was tied to a doghouse which had its door blocked so he couldn't go inside. He barked, I sloshed. He had a mammoth voice. I had a big bucket. And we went at it for a dozen times or more. Then he wagged his tail. He liked the water so long as it brought me for company. So he continued to bark.

Mischievous dogs are evasive. A trailing leash will help you to catch them—with dignity.

I liked him, too, for that matter. Certainly I didn't want to see him destroyed. But he had to learn not to bark constantly and senselessly. The only other methods I knew to accomplish that were painful ones. Some of them were out, too, since I didn't want to ruin him as a tree dog.

I cut some stout switches, set them on the back step, and went into the house. He tuned up his bark. I rushed out, bellowed "quiet!" caught him by the back of the neck and switched him. I went inside, but I was soon out again, wielding the switch and thinking, "I'm trying to save your life, stupid, so you'd better learn!"

Six switchings, and he knew that "quiet!" meant just that. I think it took two more whippings a little later to condition him properly. From there on I had a great dog who respected me and worked for me. Maybe it *was* cruel. But it saved him from a sad and early end in the pound.

I wouldn't use switches, now. Nor would I admit defeat by having a dog like TNT debarked by surgery. That's another solution, of course. I've studied dogs who have had their voice box made inoperative, and it seems to me that they enjoy their almost noiseless barking as much as the noisy ones do. But resorting to an operation is a confession of defeat, I think. It's just giving up. It doesn't help you, and certainly doesn't help him.

I've learned to use negative conditioners whenever they are necessary. I think you should accept the facts as they are: the harsher the conditioner, the more rapid the effect. You can pester and disturb your dog for days and months with weak and ineffectual methods that work slowly or not at all. Or you can teach him his lessons in a few sessions. The glowing ember needs to happen only once, and the dog who touches it knows about it for good.

Surely I don't need to tell you not to be cruel to your dog. It's a matter of degree, and it applies to the positive

121

The digger who made this hole will return. But the old-fashioned rat-trap will discourage further excavation.

reinforcements as well as to the negative ones. You certainly won't be so severe that you injure your pet. But you also won't be so gentle that, in effect, you hurt him in another way—by confusing him with ineffective methods.

To Prevent Digging

Some dogs are diggers—particularly the Terriers, of course. They were originally bred to go into burrows after game and to dig it out. And they still dig. Other breeds are less prone to this habit, but none is proof against it.

I well remember a Wire Haired Terrier I once knew. He was an inveterate digger. He would dig at anything—his kennel run, the lawn, the garden, the concrete driveway.

The family that owned him moved from the suburbs back to the city, but (largely for him, I think) they bought a house with a lovely well-planted yard—lawn and flower beds and fine flagged walks. In a day the place was ruined. There were holes all over the lawn, dirt on the walks, and the flower beds were a maze of tunnels.

The family solved the problem after a fashion. They repaired the damage and thereafter kept the dog on a leash. But for months if the owner paused by a patch of earth, the pooch would make the earth fly.

Eventually the digging habit was broken. Four years later, I heard the dog could be permitted his freedom in the park without danger of his being involved in an excavation project. He had stopped digging—so long as his owner watched him.

That's kindness—if you can call it that—and about the slowest, most painful sort of kindness I can imagine. Yet many people inflict this method on their pets. I know of a family that disposed of two dogs in three years because they dug. Both were the breed they fancied, Wire Haired Fox Terriers. I explained that Spaniels have much less tendency to dig. They bought a Cocker and it dug, too. They wouldn't take my advice. But then it turned out I wasn't so wise either. I later learned that their yard was tunneled by ground moles. Digging for moles had started all three dogs in the habit.

For a dog, digging isn't always pure mischief. Only a very stupid dog would fail to dig down to cool earth on a hot day. All of my dog runs are dug up every summer. Sometimes I find my dogs have tunneled out of sight. I forgive them.

If I were you, and had one dog instead of a hundred, I would let him spend those few unbearably hot summer afternoons in the coolest corner in the cellar. Why make him provide his own air-conditioning?

But if your dog simply loves to dig for the pleasure of seeing the flying dirt, you may have to take steps. If you

123

see him start to go underground, a stern "no!" and a slap may be enough to stop him. It often is. If that doesn't work, let him get a reasonably pleasant hole started. Then bring him into the house. Go back to his diggings, set one of those old-fashioned flat mouse traps at the bottom of it and cover it over with a little dirt. You'll be surprised at how few times he needs to be snapped before he gives up his interest in digging.

To Keep Your Dog Off the Easy Chair

Lots of little toy dogs should be encouraged to lounge in chairs and on the furniture. Some are so small and short-haired that they can't be bothersome. In fact, they are bred as lap dogs. If a woman doesn't object to having one in her lap, she can hardly mind having it on the furniture. But a large, shaggy, shedding, long-haired dog can be a real nuisance.

Incidentally (and sadly), house dogs differ from kennel dogs in one important respect: they tend to shed the year round, whereas a dog under natural light conditions sheds only once—in early summer—and gets it over with.

If your dog has been permitted to use the furniture for his bed and you want to end the habit, the solution is simply to make the furniture uncomfortable for him. How?

I have visited in homes where the chairs have always been piled on the divan and foot stools set in overstuffed chairs as a ritual when the family left the dog alone. Any dog worth his salt is cute enough to learn that he can take advantage of his owner's absence to enjoy real overstuffed comfort.

When you are at home, you can use any of the methods we have mentioned for negative reinforcement. With small dogs, a fly swatter used *every* time the pup hops up is all that is needed. Tipping chairs so that the dog falls out is good—if he happens to like a light, tippable chair. Shaking small and middlesized dogs works wonders. Your dog won't jump into a chair or onto a bed if he has learned he'll be shaken when he does. Nor will he if he knows that he will be plopped unceremoniously into a dark closet the moment he hops up.

But please remember that it is quite useless to mete out such punishment when you come home and find the dog on the furniture. He just won't understand what you are so mad about. What, then, can you do?

Certainly the simplest thing is first to confine him to one room. Then, leave only one inviting piece of furniture available to him. On that place a piece of stiff cardboard through which you have pushed three or four dozen thumb tacks or short carpet tacks. The tacks will not pierce his feet but only feel uncomfortable. Cover the cardboard neatly with a cloth. Your dog will hop right on it the minute you leave. He may hop up several times. But by then he will have learned that the sofa is not for him. Cruel? That's for you to decide.

But when you come home, don't forget about your evil plot and sit on the thing yourself. That has happened, you know.

To Stop Chewing

A lot of valuable furniture (and many pairs of slippers) has been chewed up by dogs who were otherwise relatively well-behaved. The damage is usually done by puppies from three to six months old. Their depredations often seem to be sheer mischief. But generally they are rooted in a simple need. The pups are teething, and they need something on which to sharpen their teeth and exercise their jaws. Such fellows need help, not discipline. A good big beef bone often will solve their problems—and yours. Some chewers have been made safe to leave alone simply by supplying them food in the form of large-sized dog biscuits. The biscuits are nutritious. and the pups clean their teeth on them in the bargain.

Habitual chewers are another kind of problem. I have found that they can be kept away from furniture by coating the ruined table leg or chair arm with a strong solution of bitter aloes—the stuff your grandmother once used to stop Willie from biting his fingernails.

If that doesn't stop the dog from chewing, then you will simply have to shut him up every time you leave him alone until he stops. If you catch him in the act, give him a good slapping. Or banish him to that dark closet. Or, if he is of the right size, pick him up and give him a good shaking. It's your furniture, and if he is going to live at your house, he should learn to respect it.

To Stop Car Chasing

If you think about it for a moment, you will probably remember that most of the car-chasers that you have encountered have been working dogs—Collies and Shepherds, and other dogs bred to protect flocks by driving away intruders. So they drive away cars, too. Here that big thing comes—wheels whirling and engine roaring. The dog challenges the monster. Does it stop? No. It runs away. And the dog proudly returns home, confident that it was he who scared the thing away.

That's the way it starts, and that's the way it continues. It becomes a pattern, a habit. After a while, the dog lies beside the road in wait and dashes out and barks furiously at every passing car.

Do you think this is an overstatement of the dog's attitude? If you do, I suggest that you try an experiment. The next time a dog chases your car, instead of speeding up, stop as quickly as you can. Watch the dog. He will be the very picture of confusion because the unexpected has happened to him. Here is a car that fights instead of fleeing.

If every car owner stopped instead of giving the dog the impression that the car was afraid of him and had sped off, there would be few car-chasing dogs. But since that is not likely to happen, you will have to find other ways of stopping those car-chasers. Unfortunately, you can't do it with just your own car. You need the cooperation of neighbors with their cars—because your dog will very quickly learn that though the yellow car can bite back, the black one always runs.

Car-chasing endangers the life of your dog. Sooner or later he will misjudge his distance. He also threatens the lives of the people driving past. I know a man whose dog caused two serious accidents before he fell under the wheel of a truck. I've loved dogs and worked with dogs all my life. I like these animals. And yet I've made it a principle never to endanger a human life to save that of a dog. I'm not perfect at it. When a dog rushes out at my car, my tendency is to swerve to try to miss him. But I have tried to school myself: I will not, I keep saying, sacrifice my life or that of another human being to save the life of a dog.

Now then: You have a car-chaser. There are two possibilities: either he will be hurt, or human beings will be hurt. You don't want either to happen. What do you do?

First, you get a friend to drive you past your house in his car. You sit in the back seat with a bucket of water. When your dog runs out beside the car, you slosh him full in the face with the water. You try that a few times. If he learns to avoid the black car but continues to chase others with his old enthusiasm, you find another friend with a different car. You want to teach him that *all* cars are dangerous.

You can try other treatments. Let him trail a long leash. When he comes rushing out at the car, jump out, step on the leash, and give him a great noisy whacking with a rolled newspaper.

And while you are doing all this, make a fuss about it. Shout "no" or "ho" or "git." Make a production of it—and the bigger the better.

You can use handfuls of gravel, too, flinging them hard

at the dog as you drive past. But I have always found gravel less startling than water—and besides, you might injure your dog's eyes.

Perhaps the best treatment for car-chasers that I have ever found are fire-crackers. They don't have to be big. A string of those Chinese crackers, of the very smallest kind, tossed in front of your dog will usually stop him cold. Or, if he is more persistent, you can resort to those little paper-wrapped devices called "torpedoes." They explode on impact, and if you drop a few of them in front of your car-chaser, he will be very discouraged. In many states fire-crackers are illegal (and quite properly, too), but perhaps one of your friends driving back from Florida can bring you a dozen or so of these therapeutic devices.

There's still another way to stop car-chasing—and this one goes all the way back to the old hobble that our grandfathers used to put on fence-jumping cows. You don't need anything very heavy; a broomstick will do. For an average-size dog cut it about twelve or fifteen inches long. Tie it to his collar so that it hangs in front of him horizontally, six or eight inches from the ground. He can walk around perfectly comfortably. But if he chases a car (or the paper boy on his bike), he'll come a cropper with his feet all tangled up with the stick. It works—and pretty quickly, too.

But *don't* be persuaded to use the squirt gun loaded with ammonia and water. Your dog can sneeze the stuff out of his nose. But it may seriously injure his eyes. *Don't.*

To Protect Delivery People

You want your dog to warn you when a night-time prowler comes around. You want him to bark, to raise an alarm at the right time. But you certainly don't want him to nip the postman or the milkman or the newspaper boy.

128

How do you get him to understand this nice distinction?

Well, you teach him that the delivery men are not intruders but friends. How do you do that? By the same old conditioning methods we used at the start. By using food as a reinforcement.

Again you have your dog 36-hours-hungry. Go down the street when you see the mailman coming and engage him in a small conversation. He'll be interested. Tell him, "I am going to place this bowl of food on the gate post two houses from ours. When you come along, will you please pick it up and let my dog smell it through the fence. Go through the gate and place it on the porch where he will eat it. I'd appreciate it if you would do this every morning when you see the bowl. After that I'll leave a few snacks which you can hand to him. You see, Mr. Mailman, I want him to be happy when he sees you coming."

This will work, believe me. I know, because I've suggested it to many a client who afterward told me, "My dog only barks for joy at the sight of the mailman or the milkman"—or whoever it was my clients wanted to protect. And if you put yourself in the position of a delivery man who has been annoyed by the Joneses' dog to a point where he'd like to give him a strychnine pill, you'll realize what a good thing you have done for him. He will cooperate.

About Frustration

Have you heard of dogs wrecking the inside of a car or ripping up a whole apartment? I have. I once knew a Boxer who caused $6,000 worth of damage to an apartment in the five hours he was left behind alone. That's what the insurance company paid. His owner said it should have been $9,000.

I've had the same sad experience myself. I once left a hound behind in a car while my hunting companions and I set off with two other dogs. He made a shambles of the car. He tore all the upholstery off the walls and seat, and chewed the steering wheel to a shred. We had to ride home sitting on hunting coats spread over naked springs.

Your dog will probably display a milder form of such behavior. He may jump over a kennel or yard fence when you leave him, something he never does when he knows you are home. Or he may use the sofa or a bed for his toilet.

Whatever he does, the cause is the same. He seems to be saying, "Leave me alone, will you? I'll fix you." Actually, he has no such thoughts; he is simply expressing his frustration. Not all dogs express it in the same way. Some become morose, some only bark. And when they are frustrated, it is usually the owner's fault.

Now, frustration is a vague word, and I suppose it is even more vague when it is applied to the feelings a dog has. But it seems to me to be something real, something you should guard against. Try to find out what causes it.

I have noticed that boisterous dogs are most easily driven to act in this peculiar manner. And in my experience they are almost always dogs who have been regularly permitted to have their own way, dogs who have seldom been disciplined or denied what they wanted.

The hound I mentioned—the one who ruined my car —was new to me. His owner had never been able to control him, I found out later, and that was why he had been willing to sell him to me.

If you always have taken your Doberman Pinscher for a walk when you went out, have always let him go with you when you visited friends, have always let him expect to share what you are doing—don't be surprised if he becomes frustrated when you leave him alone.

The cure of frustration, I think, is prevention. Make your dog accept your way of life. Leave him behind. Let him expect to be alone for reasonably long periods. *Don't* become a nursemaid.

Dogs With Grudges

It is strange, I suppose, to hear a veterinarian talk about dogs with grudges. Yet they do seem to have such feelings. It's amazing how many dogs are ready to attack men at any time but are always agreeable with women. There are dogs who seem to hate children and never show any animosity toward adults. And there are others who never have been known to show anything but kindness to children but are vicious with adults.

Such grudges are almost always attributed to some abuse from the kind of person a dog dislikes or fears. "Rover must have been kicked by a man when he was a pup, so now he hates men." Or, "A child must have tormented Duke when he was little, so now he hates children." Such could well be partial causes.

But that is usually not the whole story. A dog of an unreliable, chip-on-the-shoulder temperament may well have made attempts to nip or frighten adults and found that the consequences were unpleasant. But children, he discovered, had weaker defenses. So he threatens children. There are such dogs, many of them. They are sometimes dangerous, always frightening.

There is a cure for this problem, too—at least, a method that usually works. It's not infallible, and if it fails, you should, of course, get rid of any dog who seriously threatens anyone. Try having the person the dog fears or distrusts give him his food. Let him give it to him in bites, as reinforcements. Give the dog a chance before you dispose of him. If he learns to like and trust one woman or one child, he will probably accept all people of the same general size or shape or class. You can and should make some attempt to cure his fears. But don't harbor a dog who is really dangerous.

Negative reinforcements? Yes. You will need them. And if you are going to treat your dog properly, you should be prepared to use them wisely and well.

CHAPTER TEN

To Overcome Shyness

A shy dog always seems like a reproach to his owner. You want him to be outgoing, responsive, friendly, cheerful-looking. Instead, he is timid, furtive, and cowering. He hides in corners and under the furniture, slips from room to room with his tail tucked between his legs, squats down in fear even when you try to pet him.

Shyness in dogs is a bigger problem and a more common one than you may think. When I was in practice, dozens of people who really loved dogs came to me every year with some variation of the same question: "We have a wonderful dog, and we want to keep him. But he is so nervous and timid. He seems to be afraid of everybody. We've tried every way to make friends with him, but he still skulks around the house as though we were beating him. What can we do?"

Well, you can do a great deal, very easily and very quickly—if you do it the right way.

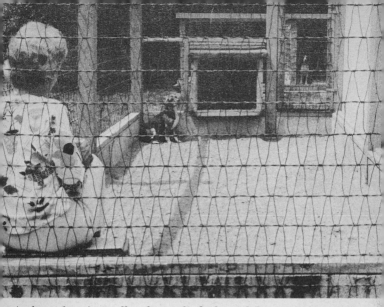

A dog that is really shy will find a place to hide even though it seems inadequate to both him and his owner.

First of all, don't pursue him. Don't chase him into a corner to pet him. Don't try to win his affection by offering him chicken à la king.

Try to understand his problem, and then provide a way for him to solve it.

To begin with, you must understand how he feels. He may have been raised in a kennel where the only human being he ever saw was the person who shoved the food pan into his cage. Nobody took the trouble to befriend him. Nobody talked to him. He may have been abused by somebody who found that even feeding him was a chore. He has never lived in a house with lights and television commercials and romping, yelling children.

Sure he's scared. And so would you be if you were in his place.

What do you do? The solution is so simple that you will wonder that you haven't thought of it yourself.

The method that we will use here is one that I've really tested. I've proved it scores of times with my own kennel dogs, and I have seen it work with hundreds of people who asked my advice on how to handle the problem with their pets. It seemed too easy to be true. So I have even had my assistant spend weeks in frightening and misusing a dog until he trembled at the sight of a man, and then tried the method on this overly shy dog as a test. Cruel? Perhaps. But I think that what we found out will show the way to get thousands of trembling dogs out of their corners.

How It's Done

Take your timid dog (36-hours-hungry, as usual) to a quiet place, free from distractions. Your garage will do. I use one of my kennel runs.

You don't need to say a word to him. For your signal you can use a large spoon with which you strike the food pan. Or you can use the dog's name, which may be better in the long run. Your object is to eliminate his fear of you (and other people) and to teach him to come to you voluntarily.

You sit on a low stool at one end of the room or enclosure. Needless to say, the dog is at the other end. Put his food pan three or four feet away from the dog. Now you are ready to start. Walk toward him, drop a tidbit into it, and tap the spoon sharply against the side. Return to your seat. He will sit cowering until he smells the food, then sneakily crawl toward it, eat the tidbit, and go back to his original hiding place in the corner. Repeat this procedure as many times as it takes to have him come forward and get the reinforcement as soon as you have tapped and moved backward. This may require all of two to five minutes, depending on how frightened and timid the dog is.

As soon as he has begun to respond promptly, move

134

the pan toward you about a foot, drop the tidbit, tap, and retire to your stool. Each time he responds, quickly move the pan another foot toward you as you drop another reinforcement and tap another tap.

Keep on doing this until you have the pan between your feet. Then move it back still a little more, under the stool. When you do that, hold your hands so that the dog will have to brush between them to obtain his reinforcement.

I can't honestly tell you how long this reconditioning will take. It depends both upon your skill and manner and on the dog's condition. I've been able to make it work in fifteen minutes with dogs that have been scandalously abused. You surely will make gratifying progress in one such short session.

You can't win his trust by pursuing him. But a little knowledge and a few minutes of patience will work wonders.

Maggie talked to this frightened dog and then offered him tidbits to reinforce his growing confidence.

He ventured closer and closer. Within ten minutes this cowering little fellow was at her feet.

But don't expect to accomplish the whole job in a single evening. Your dog won't overnight change from a whimpering thing to a gay companion. He'll probably slip back into his safe retreat. So two days later, repeat the lesson. He may seem awfully stupid at first, but in three or four minutes he will remember that you are his friend, not something he has to be afraid of. After ten minutes of the second session he should be crawling under you and permitting you to rub his ears.

At this point you may be surprised, as I have been with several of the man-shy dogs I have conditioned. Your dog may become overdemonstrative. I have had many dogs suddenly seem to realize that I am their friend and jump against me, seemingly in an effort to demonstrate that their fear of me is gone. With little dogs this is a minor problem. But with the kind of big dogs I've handled it can be a predicament. One jumped up and wrapped his leg around my arm, and I had the devil's own time to get loose. When I went out of his pen, he stood leaning against the wire trying to get closer to me. I try to avoid him now. He's big and strong, and he has never lost his conditioning.

So your dog accepts you. But he may still distrust somebody who wears a skirt, or little people who may be as afraid of him as he is of them, or the visitor with a loud voice. He may not need further training, but if he does, you know the way to handle his problem.

About that dog that my assistant deliberately abused so we could test this method: he's the one I have to dodge because he tries to knock me down with affection.

CHAPTER ELEVEN

Housebreaking

To my way of thinking, the term *housebreaking* should mean a lot more than it does to most people. It ought to include a whole category of mischievous, destructive actions. Your dog ought to be taught that you will not tolerate his chewing table legs, or ripping up the kitchen linoleum, or lying in chairs or on beds. He should be trained to stay away from the table while the family is at dinner, to eat from his own dish, and never to carry his food into other rooms.

All of these things should properly be considered part of housebreaking. But since we have already talked about ways of using negative conditioning to eliminate annoying actions such as these, we'll use the term housebreaking here in the usual sense. It will mean simply teaching your dog not to urinate or defecate except in certain permissible places.

The Basis of Housebreaking

Almost the first training that an owner attempts is to

139

This little chap is a nephew of Phoebe's. He's being restricted until he learns what newspapers mean.

teach his dog to be reliably housebroken. He is understandably in a hurry to get results. But unfortunately he often doesn't have any idea of how to begin to train the dog, or, if he does think he knows, as often as not he will try to use methods that are either ineffective or actually wrong.

To begin with, you should know more than most people seem to about the mechanics of elimination in a dog. You have noticed, of course, that a newborn puppy does not soil his bed. There is a reason. The puppy urinates and defecates only in response to the stimulation of a reflex. It may have a need to eliminate, but the need itself will not relax the muscles which retain the urine and feces. That happens only when the mother dog uses her tongue to stroke and stimulate the nerve centers which control these muscles. Thus she decides when her pups are permitted to urinate and defecate, and is therefore able to keep them and their nest clean.

So, for about his first six weeks, the puppy is conditioned to eliminate only at a touch-signal by his mother. (I've had scores of people who didn't know about this natural mechanism come to me in some alarm a day or two after they had inherited an orphan pup. The case is not one of the most difficult ones that a veterinarian encounters. A touch or so with a wad of cotton and the problem is solved.) After these first few weeks, the hormone which triggers the mother dog's instinct to keep the pup clean begins to dwindle. She no longer gives the pup that kind of care. But during that time the pup has been firmly conditioned not to soil his bed. He has also learned to go exploring beyond his nest. He soon discovers that though it is wrong to soil his bed, elimination is permitted outside the nest. How does he know that he is in the proper place? Partly by what he sees, perhaps. But mostly, many experiments have shown, by what he *feels* —and most of what he feels he senses through the pads of his feet.

That simple fact is the key to easy housebreaking.

For years most of my pups have been raised in hutches a couple of feet off the ground with a good-sized wire-bottom pen attached. They learn almost immediately that elimination is permitted over this inch-square wire mesh —and, incidentally, if you try one of these pens, you will find that they are the cleanest and most sanitary way you've ever found to handle a litter of pups.

There are, however, small and unexpected dangers to guard against. A friend of mine who lives in the South once raised a litter of Cocker Spaniels in such a pen. He sold the puppies, and it happened that a good many of them went to people who had one-pipe furnaces in their homes—the kind that sends the heat up through a grating in the floor. The pups all discovered the grating—with, my friend reported, distressing results.

What you will probably do is to spread newspapers in a good wide area around the puppy's bed. He'll go exploring. Since his mother has stopped stimulating his reflexes, he'll eliminate on the paper. Nothing bad happens to him. He feels the paper under his feet, finds that that means a safe place for his toilet, and is newly conditioned. That's the whole story. The question is how to get your pup reliably trained to this system.

How It's Done

The first thing you need is a proper bed for the pup. Don't be too generous. He's going to grow a lot, I know, but you can give him that nice big bed for a Christmas present later. He'll get along better right now with something smaller and less lavish.

The thing to remember now is that he has already been conditioned not to soil his bed. The trick is to provide him with one which is just large enough to let him sleep comfortably curled up—stretched out is the position for sunning himself—but one which has no room in it for a toilet.

Having provided the right bed, you will make provisions for keeping him in or on his bed except at certain times. You can do that with a light chain that is attached with swivels to his collar and to a hook in the wall behind the bed. Or you can make a light wire-mesh box that fits over the bed when he's in it. I prefer the latter, since it gives the dog more freedom. At first, when you go out and during the night, you must make sure he stays in his bed. When you do let him out—and this you will do, of course, at decently frequent intervals—be sure there is plenty of paper around his bed and that he stays on it. He will step onto the paper, relieve himself, associate the feeling of the paper underfoot with the relief. He is beginning to be conditioned.

From here on the key to successful housebreaking is simply repetition. I can't tell you precisely how long it will take. I've had dogs reliably housebroken in a week. Others have taken twice as long. Once in a long while you will encounter a pup who seems to be determined to

142

The pen has disappeared, the newspaper has moved to the back door and started to slide out under it.

Not much paper is left here—not enough for a proper toilet. Your dog will probably complain about it.

be a real continuing problem—but only once in a long while, in my experience.

The problems usually arise with new and inexperienced owners who have the mistaken notion that if they *show* the dog what they want him to do, he will understand. Unfortunately, he won't. Housebreaking, therefore, is relatively slow simply because the *need* to eliminate has to be fulfilled only a few times a day—six or eight at the most. Nevertheless, by the end of the first week your dog should be pretty dependably conditioned to paper, provided that you have arranged matters so that the paper covers every place he can go when he steps out of bed.

You won't want to keep your pet tied or shut in his bed for long periods. Instead, once he has learned the uses of paper, you can provide a limited paper-covered area around his bed for his use. I've known people who

When the door is opened, your pup will be pleased to see that the paper has reappeared half way across the porch.

used an old baby pen for the purpose. Four expandable window screens securely hooked together at the corners will serve the same purpose. Be sure that you cover all of the available toilet space within the area. After a week, it is generally safe to remove the pen. But keep paper spread over the same area. After you are sure that the dog knows what the paper is for, you can move it to the place in the bathroom or cellar or kitchen that you want the dog to use as his toilet.

If you live in the suburbs, or if you have a yard connected with your house in the city, you'll want to carry the pup's education a bit further. Little by little you will move the paper until it is just inside the back door. Leave it there for a few days until you are sure your pup knows where to find it. Then put it outside the door—but leave a corner of it sticking underneath as a reminder. Your dog will find this meager remnant too small for his pur-

The paper keeps receding. It slides under the porch door and is pinned down in a proper place on the lawn.

Little by little the paper disappears. Just after this picture was taken it vanished entirely.

poses. As soon as you see that he has encountered a problem, let him out. After you have helped him a few times, he may scratch at the door as a signal. Or he may bark to ask to go out. When he does, always open the door for him immediately.

Now that you have the paper out on the stoop, you will begin to move it toward the spot that you want the dog to use. Don't try any short cuts. If your pup has been well-conditioned to paper, you can take him for a long walk —and he'll wait until he is back in the house to use the paper. So move the paper gradually to the place where you want the dog to eliminate. After he has learned where to go, you can begin to reduce the amount of paper provided each day until finally only a scrap is left. But by time the area you have chosen will itself be a substitute signal, and your dog will be conditioned to the outdoors.

There are, as always, chances to make mistakes. Suppose you train your pup to use a grassy corner of your yard as a toilet. He becomes conditioned, you remember, to the *feel* of the place underfoot. It is quite possible that the nap of your living-room rug will seem to him quite like the well-mown grass in the yard—and the result may be the same. Either you will be careful about the surface of the spot which you have chosen as a toilet for your pup, or you will provide acceptable substitutes (other than the rug) indoors.

There are ways to do that, too. A friend of mine had a dandy little Fox Terrier called Duz. His children teethed on her ear. She regularly provided litters of pups to the utter delight of the small fry. She was next to perfect— but she never did learn to distinguish a fine gray rug from a good green lawn. My friend disputed this matter with her for quite a while. Then he decided to join her. Back in the corner of the kitchen he put one of those sisal or cocoa mats that usually lie outside the door where the kids arrive with muddy feet. Duz agreed that the mat was more like grass than the rug. From then on Duz did everything on the mat. The children—her master and mistress—were assigned the small chore of hosing the mat off every day or so. Duz died at a ripe old age—and so far as I know, she never really did understand the difference between a mat and a lawn. But the rugs in the house still look good, and my friends seem likely to live happily ever after.

In this chapter—and in those that went before—you have had the nub of the natural training method. After years of trial and error with other training systems, this one seems to me to be the easiest, the quickest, the kindest that you can use.

When you use the natural training method, you aban-

148

on force. You use the dog's own needs to train him. You reinforce your dog's proper responses directly, immediately, and in a way that encourages him to work more industriously. You discourage destructive behavior, when necessary, with negative reinforcements. In short, you use the obvious, effective methods available to you to make your pet the responsive, responsible dog that he should be.

Isn't that what you want of him?

Index

SAVE MONEY . . . TAKE ADVANTAGE OF OUR SPECIAL PRICE OFFER!

Award books retail at prices from 60¢ to 95¢ per title wherever paperbound books are sold. You may order any of these books directly from us at special reduced prices. Use the special order coupon on the last page.